Praise for Zero Frequency

«We all want a balance between work and family, between rest and activity, between financial success and a sense of meaning. Mabel has provided a practical, yet profound, manual for achieving a meaningful, balanced life. This book will transform the way you think about challenges and show you how to harness its power».

DON MIGUEL RUIZ, #1 *New York Times* best-selling author
of The Four Agreements

«A healthy life requires creating a healthy rhythm in your life. In *Zero Frequency,* Mabel Katz will show you how to use your inner power to create and sustain your own unique life rhythm so that your life flows with ease and grace».

MICHAEL BERNARD BECKWITH, Founder & Spiritual Director, Agape International Spiritual Center and author
of Life Visioning y *Spiritual Liberation*

«I've had the good fortune to be exposed to the tremendous power of Ho'oponopono. Now, Mabel Katz has opened that power to everyone in *Zero Frequency.* This book is a must-read!».

MARCI SHIMOFF, #1 *New York Times* best-selling author
of Happy for No Reason

«*Zero Frequency* is a gateway to a more conscious, meaningful life. There's a reason the world's most accomplished people incorporate spirituality into their lives to help them achieve peak performance, to stay calm under pressure, and to have balance in their lives. This book shows you why.».

JANET BRAY ATTWOOD, *New York Times* best-selling author
of The Passion Test

«This profound and beautiful book will take you into the meaning and purpose of your life by providing practical tools for connecting with what matters to you most. Rarely have I seen a book that can take you so deeply into a process to achieve your dreams for a truly fulfilling life».

MARCIA WIEDER, CEO, Dream University
and best-selling author

«Eureka! Exactly the book I've been looking for. I loved Zero Frequency for its straightforward approaches and heartwarming stories for a happy and fulfilling life».

PAT BURNS, Co-founder of the *Orange County Children's Book* Festival and GRAND Magazine Journalist

«Mabel is a natural storyteller and purveyor of elegant wisdom that immediately touches people's hearts. Her genius is spinning an elegant yarn that connects us to simple truths that inspire us to be the best we can be».

PETER MONTOYA,
author of *The Brand Called You*

«Mabel has put together a powerful strategy for anyone to step into a better life - I'm proof! After a business fallout it wasn't very long until I was prospering. Apply what you learn in *Zero Frequency* and you too can come out on top, regardless of what life throws at you».

MATTHEW DAVID HURTADO,
The Minister of Allowing

«¡Zero Frequency* is an insightful and inspiring book! It teaches us to create more happiness, success and peace in our lives. I highly recommend it!».

GARY QUINN,
life coach and author of The Yes Frequency

First Edition
The Zero Frequency® service mark and trademark are registered marks of Your Business, Inc.
All other trademarks and registered trademarks are the property of their respective owners.
US Copyright Registration Number: TXu 2-171-165

Names:	Katz, Mabel, author
Title:	Zero Frequency® The easiest way to peace, happiness, and abundance / Mabel Katz.
Description:	[Woodland Hills, California] : [Your Business Press], [2020] "Based on Ho'oponopono"-- Cover.
Identifiers:	ISBN: 978-1-7333317-2-2 (paperback)	978-1-7333317-3-9 (ebook) LCCN: 2020905992
Subjects:	LCSH: Ho'oponopono.	Self-realization.	Self-actualization (Psychology) Success -- Psychological aspects.	Peace of mind.	Happiness. Stress management.	Problem solving.	Self-help techniques. Spirituality.	Conduct of life.
Classification:	LCC: BF637.S4 K389 2020	DDC: 158.1-- dc23 10 9 8 7 6 5 4 3 2 1

© Book Design and Cover Layout by CB Messer
© Photography for Cover: Depositphotos.com/elenathewise
© Publishing consultant: Geoff Affleck
© Publisher's Cataloging-in-Publication data

Published by Your Business Press | P.O. Box 427 | Woodland Hills, CA 91365
zerofrequency.com | *mabelkatz.com*

MABEL **KATZ**

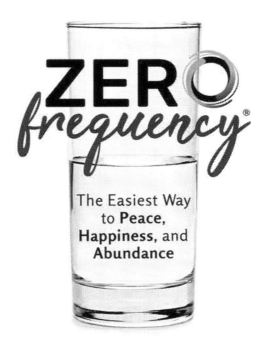

ZERO
frequency®

The Easiest Way
to **Peace**,
Happiness, and
Abundance

Your Business Press

To my mother, Sara Naiman,
who passed away as I was writing this book.
She was the wind beneath my wings
and will forever be in my heart. Who I am today
is because of what I have received from her.
This book is for you, Mom, with my greatest love.

Contents

꧁

Acknowledgments

I created and presented my first *Zero Frequency*® training in 2010. Since then I have wanted to write this book, but, due to my busy schedule traveling around the world giving my trainings, it always seemed impossible. I want to give special thanks to my friend Deborah Barnet who encouraged me all these years to write it, until finally, in the summer of 2018, I told myself that I had to find the way.

So, I hired Ruth Klein as my writing coach and Ruth brought Eliana Golden to edit to keep me on track and accountable. I actually wanted to hire a ghost writer, but they kept encouraging me: "Keep writing, you are doing great." They understood the importance of the message I was trying to convey in this crazy mission of mine, that I wanted to help people transform not only their personal but also their professional lives and make this world a better and happier place!

When I thought the manuscript was finished, Anjanette Harper showed up and helped me to tweak it and pieced it all together. She was a game-changer for me. It gave me the added value, and "new ideas" that this book needed to become the book I am proud to present here today. Thank you all.

My heartfelt thanks to Francesc Prims who worked with me on the book a couple of years ago when I thought I'd write it in Spanish. I decided to write it in English, the language in which my inspiration flows best. Still, Francesc, your collaboration, talent, and ideas have contributed to the book and are reflected in it. Also, a BIG thanks to Bill Apablasa for all his input, advice and support.

Thank you to the ancient Hawaiian art of problem-solving known as Ho'oponopono. It transformed my life! Thank you to Morrnah Simeona for updating this art to our modern times.

A huge thank you to my teacher, Dr. Ihaleakalá Hew Len, for the twelve years I spent under your tutelage and as your apprentice. Your guidance had prepared me to do the work I've been doing in the world and led to the birth of Zero Frequency®.

Thank you to my students around the world for your commitment and trust. My organizers around the world and my team: Thank you for your dedication, efforts, love, and for believing in my message and for helping me spread it.

Last but not least, THANK YOU to my amazing sons, Jonathan and Lyonel, and my daughter-in-law, Corinne, for your unconditional love, support, and reassurance. You are the blessing in my life and the best gift God has given me. Thank you for encouraging me to keep going, no matter what.

Introduction

✣

«Why do I struggle to reach my dreams?».

"What will it take for me to finally achieve financial abundance?"

"Why am I still unhappy?"

It usually happens. At one of my live events, someone will ask me a version of one—or all—of those three questions. I've answered them thousands of times. When this happens, I smile. It does not bother me to hear the same question over and over again. We are family, you see. We are the human family and we are all looking for the same things: a sense of purpose, passion fulfilled, enough money to enjoy life, peace in our relationships, peace in the world, peace in our own hearts and minds.

Most likely, you've asked yourself these same questions. Maybe you are reading this because you tried to find your own way and feel frustrated with the results you've achieved so far. I hope you found this book because you still believe it's possible for you to be truly happy and fulfilled. Could it be that you know deep down that there is a simpler path toward what you want?

Whatever the reason you picked up this book, know you are not alone. As I tell the lovely people who ask me the same heartfelt questions at my Zero Frequency® seminars and workshops: There is an easier way. In fact, I found the easiest way to do it.

Some of you may already know me through my life-long work with Ho'oponopono, the ancient Hawaiian art of problem-solving, which for me has been a philosophy of life, one that has nourished and sustained me in both good times and challenging times. In the beginning, the ancient practice involved gathering the entire family, and, in the presence of a moderator, each member would ask the others for forgiveness. Hawaiian healer Morrnah Nalamaku Simeona updated Ho'oponopono for modern times so that it could be practiced alone. Morrnah said, "The main purpose of this process is to discover the Divinity within oneself. The Ho'oponopono is a profound gift, which allows one to develop a working relationship with the Divinity within and learn to ask that in each moment, our errors in thought, word, deed or action be cleansed. The process is essentially about freedom, complete freedom from the past."

I have studied and practiced Ho'oponopono and taught its principles for more than twenty years now. I will continue to do so with a grateful heart. It is through my study of Ho'oponopono that I discovered the easiest way to peace, happiness and abundance.

In my own life, I experienced the transformational power of practicing Ho'oponopono. In times of pain and uncertainty, this process held me as though I was a young child and carried me to my true self. When I let go and trusted this path, everything became easier. Money flowed to me. Opportunities showed up in my inbox. I enjoyed harmony in my close relationships. My days were full of work I loved so much it did not seem like work. Worry and anxiety eased. The past no longer haunted me, and I no longer engaged in drama or strife. Failure ceased to exist. What I experienced in my own life was remarkable. What others who walked this path experienced astounded me and filled my heart with joy. I will share some of these stories with you in this book so you can see the power of Ho'oponopono.

But this book will tell a new story.

You see, on my journey, I realized that there was a need to present truth in a more practical, modern way—one that would simultaneously speak to the mind and the heart and perhaps cut through many of the mind-traps that prevent us from experiencing truth. Thus, Zero Frequency® was born.

Since I began teaching my method, I have given trainings and workshops in thirty-eight countries, in eighty-five cities. Through these events, my books and other outreach, I have helped millions of seekers all over the world. Every day I receive messages from people who, through the practice, live more often and deeply at Zero Frequency® and have experienced that which had previously seemed elusive to them: peace, happiness and abundance. And it is my hope that Zero Frequency® will help you as well, forever ending your struggle to achieve your dreams. It is my wish that you will finally encounter the happiness and peace you deserve.

So, what is Zero Frequency®? Across many continents, I have been asked this question by many people, from the very young to the very old. Simply put,

Zero Frequency® is our natural way or condition, who we really are. It's the magic way of living twenty-four/seven in inspiration, freed from the chains of all our subconscious programming and all our preconceived ideas, memories and beliefs. When we are at Zero, we are our authentic selves, able to access our true talents and natural gifts. We are always happy and at peace when we are not dependent on anything or anybody outside ourselves. We are in the flow; what is right and perfect for us comes to us easily and effortlessly.

Those who ascribe to numerology believe that numbers have vibrations. The number zero resonates with the vibrations of eternity, flow and wholeness. It also represents choice. It is the alpha, which is the beginning, and the omega, the highest. Zero is also the symbol of infinity, and it is believed that it brings us closer to God. Zero is also the symbol of nothingness; we often perceive that to be negative in nature. That is so far from the truth! In actuality, it is in this nothingness that we experience an absence of all of the memories, thoughts, beliefs and actions that have held us back. It is in this nothingness that all answers are revealed.

At Zero, you connect to the wisdom of the Universe. More than that, you are one with the

Universe. At Zero, you are not afraid. You do not think too much or worry. You don't fear failure, rejection or any specific outcome. Letting go of how you will get there, you move confidently toward your heart's desire. You trust and allow the frequency itself to take you places and to open doors for you—doors you never imagined you could walk through. At Zero, you are your own rhythm. You know you have no limits; answers and solutions just pop into your mind. You know things and you're not sure how you know them. At Zero, you are truly happy and at peace with yourself, your loved ones, your community and the world.

Zero Frequency® will captivate you, open up your heart, and change and enrich your spiritual and material life forever. It will provide you with the missing key by which to unlock the psychological state necessary to manifest the life of your dreams and remain at peace.

I suspect that you are here because some deeper part of you knows there is more to the world than what you can touch with your hands or see with your eyes. This seeking and questioning part of you is the real you—the one that lives beyond the masks of nationality, religion, politics, career, bank accounts and all the other illusions of life. This part of you is who you truly are—a Soul who has come into this world with a purpose and a specific destiny. As the great Indian mystic Osho once said, "You are here because you have something to fulfill, some message to be delivered, some work that has to be completed. You are not here accidentally—you are here meaningfully."

Once you have the awareness to understand this truth and the courage to embrace it, it then becomes your mission to discover what your purpose is. This will only happen when you first discover who you really are. The two go hand in hand. One cannot exist without the other.

This search begins and ends at Zero.

Right now, you might be thinking, "This doesn't sound easy at all." After all, up until now, discovering who you are has not been a simple task! I am hoping you will trust me to see this book through to the end so that you can experience Zero Frequency® yourself. Remember, it doesn't have to be hard if you choose to connect and live at Zero. You don't have to learn a new language or sacrifice your life. For this path to work for you, you don't have to understand how it works. You don't need anything special to practice it and you can't do it wrong. You just have to practice it. The easiest way is simply the easiest way.

You may also question whether Zero Frequency®
is compatible with your spiritual belief system. When
I use the word God in this book, I am referring to the
universal creative source. Some people call it a higher
power. Some people call it spirit. As Julia Cameron
said in her book, *The Artist's Way,* this creative source is
like electricity: You don't have to believe in electricity
to use it. When I tell people that we all talk about the
same thing, that's good news. There is one truth, but
there are different ways of exploring it. I found the
easiest way. Does this way work for everybody? Yes. Is
this way for everybody? No. A lot of people are still
addicted to suffering and blaming and complaining.
Some people say they want to change, but they don't.
I think you do want to change. I think you do want to
follow the easiest way, and I think you're ready.

This book speaks to the heart. As you read it,
you may find yourself slipping into the state of Zero
Frequency®. You may feel peaceful and creative. This
book will take you on an inner journey and teach
you how to choose to go back to Zero moment by
moment. So enjoy the ride, and may it inspire you to
learn further and cultivate being at Zero and living in
this space.

But, please know, this is not a journey that goes from Point A to Point B in one straight line. This is not a follow-the-recipe-spirituality where one suddenly finds herself sitting under the Bodhi Tree. Zero is much subtler. It is mysterious and elusive and, like the Now itself, will be found and lost on a moment-by-moment basis. Zero is pure potentiality. It is the beginning: the very moment when an idea emerges or when a new thought pops into your head. Zero comes before we start counting and before something grows. It is not the harvest; it is the seed.

While you can certainly read from one chapter to the next, don't expect Zero to happen on the last page of the last chapter. Zero can happen at any time, in any given moment. Trust, let go, connect and allow the power of Zero to transform your life. Are you ready to be reborn and connect with all your potential?

I celebrate your awakening, along with your commitment to take responsibility for your spiritual growth: your happiness, peace, awareness, freedom and abundance. You are about to take an incredible journey to consciousness. And I am happy to play a small part.

Let's begin.

Chapter 1

Trust—The Universe
Is Waiting for You

*When you follow your natural path, you find your flow,
and you attract the resources you need to attract
your full potential.*
Anonymous

Five days after Hurricane Maria hit Puerto Rico,
José Andrés, a James Beard Award-winning chef
arrived on the island on one of the first commercial
planes that landed after the disaster. Andrés was there
to feed as many people as possible. He didn't have
a plan, he hadn't thought through a strategy, and he
didn't know if he would have enough resources. And
yet, in the weeks that followed, José and his fellow
chefs fed 3.6 million people. He didn't think. He
didn't set goals. He just started cooking.

In an article in *Bon Appetit,* Andres said, "I think the biggest lesson is also the simplest one: When you find yourself up against a challenge, just start moving. Maybe it's not profound; it's not a lesson that will win a Nobel Prize, but it's a lesson that will make an opportunity out of a problem. If you try to tackle everything all at once, you will stall, you will freeze, you will have a meeting to establish another meeting, because you are trying to come up with ways to postpone action. We didn't meet. We just began cooking. A thousand meals the first day, then doubled the number every day. Before we knew it, we were at 150,000 meals a day!"

Imagine! Millions of people in need fed because one man didn't stop to think, or plan or set goals. He just started cooking! Amazing feats can be accomplished when we follow our Inspiration, let go and take action. We keep trying to fix problems such as homelessness with thinking and planning. What if we just started *doing*? It is the fretting and planning that hold us back from making big things—impossible things—happen.

People are always amazed when I tell them that I do not set goals. "How do you get anything done?" they ask. In our fast-paced, achievement-oriented society, that seems like a fair question. In North America, most believe that we must plot our futures and strive to achieve our goals and dreams. An entire industry exists to help us become better at managing our time at planning and setting goals, at creating treasure boards visualizing our ideal future. I know people are surprised when I tell them I don't set goals. I know what they are *really* wondering is, "If you don't set goals, how did you come to live such a happy life?" They see my contentment and they want to ask, "How did you reach this peace?" They see my books, my speaking tours and other work I do. They yearn to understand, "How have you achieved this?"

All of this—my happy life, my contentment, my work around the world—is possible for anyone. I'm not special, or chosen, or smiled upon any more than any other human on this planet, including you. Your life depends on your decisions. I decided to take responsibility and stop blaming and complaining. I became more humble. I realized I didn't know as much I thought I did. I stopped paying attention to other people's opinions and judgments. I forgave. I realized I didn't have to be perfect and started accepting myself just the way I was. I paid more attention to my heart's desires and opened my mind and chose to let go and trust. If you are looking for the easiest way to happiness, peace and abundance, I highly recommend this path.

I don't set goals. I do not spend a lot of time planning or strategizing next steps. I enjoy living in the present. I do not have a vision board and I do not use affirmations. Despite all of this, I am the happiest I have ever been. I am doing the work I love. I am on my life mission. I have no money worries. I am not concerned about my next venture. My relationships are harmonious and fulfilling. Stressful situations pass quickly. Life is easy. Life is wonderful. These are bold statements, I know. Yet, they are all true. They are true because I practice the ancient Hawaiian spiritual path to problem-solving, Ho'oponopono, the easiest way. They are true because I live at Zero Frequency®.

If you've read more than your share of personal-growth books, you already know that sometimes it's not easy to do the work they ask of you. They require a lot from us and yield inconsistent results. When things don't work out despite our best efforts and most earnest planning, we blame ourselves. We think we must not be doing something right or we must not be ready to receive all that we desire. None of that is true. Acclaimed author and teacher Michael Beckwith says that affirmations force your subconscious mind to focus on lies because you are affirming something you don't yet have. He also says that affirmations are "Kindergarten tools" and that to "graduate," we just have to be ourselves. Zero Frequency® is a completely different approach than using affirmations. It is a loving approach and is the easiest way to truth.

You *are* enough. You are ready to receive. The Universe is waiting! Time to graduate. Time to be your authentic self!

According to Joe Vitale, author of *Zero Limits,* when we strive to achieve something, either through personal-growth exercises such as affirmations or through practical goal-setting, we get the illusion that we are in control. And yet, when we give up that control to the Universe, we get better outcomes. You see, when we set goals and make strategic plans, we are operating with the belief that we are the creators. We think and act as if it is up to us alone to make our dreams a reality. While this is a more positive and powerful approach than bemoaning the state of our lives and comparing our circumstances to others', it is not the easiest way to find true peace, happiness and abundance. The easiest way is to take it one step further and co-create with the part of us that knows better. How do we do that? We realize we don't know as much as we think we know. We let go and trust that the Universe knows what is right and the best way to achieve it. We observe, let go, stay at Zero and allow the path to become clear.

In a business seminar I presented in Holland, someone sarcastically asked me: "So you don't do projections, no business plans?"

My response was: "Would you be willing to prepare a different kind of business plan? Maybe different than the conventional one, or the one we 'know' is the correct one? Perhaps a business plan that comes from Inspiration rather than knowledge? Perhaps there are other ways? Maybe you don't even need a plan to get the loan for your business."

I shared with them that I had met a couple in Israel who had created an interesting personal-growth training program based on a game with special cards. They said that they got their first business loan due to their "enthusiasm." The banker told them that they did not qualify for the loan, but he would grant it anyway because they had such a belief in their product and they were so enthusiastic. So maybe it is our love and trust in what we do and what we have to offer that works even better than a business plan!

If you give up planning and setting goals, you will set yourself free. God has more in store for you than you can ever imagine or dream. In the beginning, letting go is the unknown. It's uncomfortable. You will have to be willing to get out of your comfort zone (the known). However, when you practice and practice and let go and start seeing the results, you will keep letting go and trusting. You will like it—you will like it because suddenly doors will open effortlessly. All you will have to do is walk through them. You will be in that perfect flow.

Make Illogical Decisions

In 1997, I was working as a tax accountant at a large Certified Public Accountant (CPA) firm in Los Angeles. I enjoyed professional success and made a lot of money, working part-time, in a business dominated by men. What more could I have asked for?

At that time, however, I was going through a divorce after a twenty-year marriage. I had a secure job and a predictable salary; the logical thing to do would have been to continue at the CPA firm. Instead, I decided to open my own accounting business. This impulse came out of nowhere and was not a wise move to even consider.

Some people advised me against leaving my job, but I knew I had to trust guidance from the Universe. What happened next surprised all of the naysayers in my life. My accounting practice became successful almost overnight. Clients came to me out of nowhere. Without any effort from me, my phone started ringing with people who needed help. They came to me through word of mouth. I know it may seem unbelievable. At the time, even I was in awe of what was happening. A small part of me still wondered if letting go and co-creating with God would work *every time*. Was this just a fluke?

I have to tell you that what finally convinced me was an experience I had with clients. Most of the clients who came to me were encumbered with tax problems. They were being audited and needed me to represent them before the Internal Revenue Service (IRS). Some of my clients were sure that they would end up owing tens of thousands of dollars. Normally, this is a highly stressful situation that can have dire consequences. Yet, I didn't get caught up in the worry or expectation. I completely let go and stayed at Zero as much as possible. The results I saw when applying this technique during those audits were miraculous. Even the most difficult audits came through with flying colors. The auditor would suddenly discover an error from a previous year that worked in my client's favor or realize a rule had not been applied properly, which would let my client off the hook.

You see, when you let go and let God, amazing things happen! Unfortunately, most of the time, we are involved emotionally and/or have expectations. We worry and think about our problems obsessively. I always got great results in audits because I was not emotionally involved, nor did I have expectations. So, I was able to let go one hundred percent and get positive results for my clients every time.

By 2003, I had been studying for a few years with the Hawaiian spiritual teacher Dr. Ihaleakalá Hew Len and practicing Ho'oponopono. Taking advantage of the financial security my accounting practice was giving me, I started my own radio and TV shows for the Latino community in Los Angeles. For the first time in my life I allowed myself the freedom to dive into my desire to be an author and speaker. I had finally discovered my real passion: to share with others what had helped me. I had enjoyed my work as a freelance accountant, but that was not my passion; that was "work." I had chosen that profession earlier in life based on what others told me I had to do because I had an innate talent for numbers.

What started at the local level began to expand with the help of the shows and teleclasses. In 2008, although I was in significant debt due to the money invested in the shows and had no savings, I decided to let go of my accounting office. People thought I was crazy to close my practice. As soon as I made that "illogical" decision, I started receiving invitations from everywhere. I began to travel around the world to conduct seminars and conferences in which I shared my simple method to attain personal and business success and financial freedom. I should mention that at the time I started conducting these seminars and conferences, I was not making even close to the six-digit annual income I had made with my accounting business. My intellect, always practical, would have never made that decision! And so, years after making the "illogical" decision to start my own accounting practice, again I felt compelled to let go, although financially it seemed really crazy! I closed my accounting office and dove wholeheartedly into my passion. Once again, I trusted my heart. I let go, and I let God.

I had another opportunity to start fresh, to start from Zero, one of the best gifts the Universe could have given me! Please know, I had never taken any training in public speaking or writing books. To this day, people from all over the world are constantly telling me how much my books changed their lives. They have been translated and published in almost twenty languages. The e-mails with invitations from all over the world and offers to license my books never stopped coming since I left my accounting career back in 2008. My seminar schedule requires me to travel to all continents. Need I say more? All of this came about because of the "illogical" decisions I had taken.

You have to believe in yourself. The people who think your dreams are silly or your decisions are crazy are simply putting voice to your own internal doubts. They show you your own fears. When they say, "Are you sure?" that is you questioning your own certainty. The cure for that is not to engage with people who doubt you. Just focus on the present, let go, and trust. It's okay if you don't have all of the answers. It's okay if you don't know how you are going to realize your dreams. Leave that to the Universe. I realize you may not know how to do that yet. That's okay. This book will show you how.

I am Argentinean and Jewish. I consider myself to be an intellectual and I am well educated. I have two degrees in Argentina (CPA and License in Business Administration). My astrological sun sign is Virgo, which makes me down to earth and good at seeing and foreseeing all the negatives. My story is a good example of how someone can change and become less arrogant and more humble. If I learned how to say, "I don't know," that means anyone can do it!

What Does Zero Frequency® Feel Like?

When I was an accountant, I would get up in the morning and think, *Oh, my goodness, I have so much to do! How am I going to get all of this done?* I was always stressed, always pushing for more, always worried about outcomes.

One morning, I was scheduled to go to a client's office, but I had a lot of work that day and needed to reschedule. The problem was, I couldn't do that because I had already rescheduled once. I chose not to worry about it. I let go, and, within minutes, the phone rang. It was my clients canceling their appointment and asking to set up another time!

At Zero Frequency®, things get resolved and stress lasts but a moment. Once I started living at Zero, my days became easier. This is what happens when you let go. The Universe takes over and organizes for you. Suddenly, instead of feeling overwhelmed, you feel calm. Everything falls into place. In fact, everything organizes better than it would have if you had tried to make your dreams happen. Doors open that you did not expect to open, that you didn't even know existed. This is how I was able to transform my life. This is how millions of Puerto Rican people in desperate need were fed. This is how your own dreams will be fulfilled.

In today's hectic and complicated world, it's easy to always be on the go—moving, rushing and heading somewhere. We have GPS systems in our cars, maps on our phones and to-do lists in our pockets. And because we can cross off all the things we've accomplished, we convince ourselves that we're productive and even compliment ourselves on our ability to do many things at once. And, of course, we need to get things done to raise our families, pay the mortgage and keep the boss happy. But what we cannot do is always be looking for the green lights in our lives. We need to look for the yellow and red lights that allow us to pause and Be. We cannot be afraid of the peace and the silence that allows us to be with ourselves.

Osho often talked about how, on our journey through life, we only see arrows: places to go and directions to take. Most of us never notice another symbol along the way: the zero mark. He was on a walk in the woods and he came across a stone with a zero mark on it and he realized it meant he had arrived at his destination. Unfortunately, our minds don't allow us to see this. The mind only sees arrows.

It's up to each of us to find the zero marks in our own lives—to realize that we need to stop and pause. These symbols are everywhere and not just stones on the road, but moons, circles, yellow lights and red lights. It could be a sunset. Zeros are everywhere. There is a reason that the word "now" has the letter "o" in the middle. It is the symbol for zero, nothingness and knowing. And it is only in the now—the present moment—that we will realize that there's no other place we need to be than precisely where we are.

In his book, *The Beginning of the Beginning,* Osho writes how the important part of the house is the door, where there is empty space that allows you to enter and leave the house. He also uses the example of a water jug: "You fill a water vessel—where does the water fill? In the empty space of the vessel, of course. So the vessel actually comprises the empty space, whereas the walls of the vessel merely surround the empty space within... So the empty space within the pot is the important part of the pot." What is invisible—the empty space—is what will enable us to bring our awareness and divinity to life, to live more at Zero Frequency®. It is what makes all things possible. This is what Zero feels like.

When you are at Zero, you get up in the morning and, even if you notice there are issues to deal with that day, you don't worry because you are above all of your problems. You perceive situations differently, as if you are an observer; you are not emotionally attached to any outcome. You engage less and you choose your battles. When you are at Zero Frequency®, you are happy for no reason and at peace no matter what. You see with God's eyes, not through the filters of your past experiences and perceived limitations.

At Zero, you make decisions consciously, not reactively. You are more present and you pay more attention. As Michael Singer says, you are aware that you are aware. You now know there is something more for you, a bigger plan, and that you are not here by chance. You know everything is part of the plan and everything is perfect.

I know this is true because this is my life. This is also the life of the tens of thousands of people who practice connecting to Zero Frequency®. As you begin to connect to Zero, be patient with yourself. This is the easiest way, but you may need some time to experience it fully. It is like going back to the gym and working on muscles you haven't focused on in years. The more your practice (work out), the easier it gets. With time, being at Zero becomes natural, like breathing. It will become automatic.

When you touch a tuning fork, you can hear the sound of the vibration. Did you know that, if there is another tuning fork close by with that same frequency, it will vibrate and sound without you touching it? And, if other tuning forks around have a higher frequency, they will not be affected. This is very important information. We attract and are affected by things in our same frequency. If we don't like what we are attracting, we need to elevate our frequency. This is exactly what we are doing when we connect to Zero. As you change, everything changes.

Going back to Zero is a choice you make moment by moment. As you read this book, you will learn many ways to connect. Simply turn to the Connect to Zero Frequency® section at the end of most chapters. At first, you may think *this is not working.* Keep going! Keep practicing! The more you let go and trust, the more rewards you will receive.

Your Only Job Is to Be Happy

When I was still searching for my path, I remember telling my sons, who were very young at the time, that their only job in life was to be happy. I didn't understand what I was saying then, but now I do. When you are happy, you are in the flow. It is the perfect flow that takes you to the right place, at the perfect time, all the time, with all the right people working alongside you. Suddenly you are "lucky." Things start to work for you, and you find the time, energy and willingness to do whatever it takes. When you are happy, you are at Zero. You stop being an obstacle in your own life because you stop thinking and reacting emotionally. You are ever-present, free, open and aware.

Zero Frequency® is an experience. At Zero, Inspiration (God) shows up, offering you perfect ideas and solutions. Once you start trusting this Universal Truth, you can relax, knowing that you are not alone. You have the support of the entire Universe. Now you know you can choose Zero. You are at long last free to enjoy and experience the mystery and magic of life.

When you allow the universe to show you, you find out who you really are, you find your purpose and mission, and you feel great about yourself. You realize that life is much more important than you think it is. Getting up and going to work, watching TV and going to sleep—that's not living. Life is an exciting opportunity, and we are all very important people. We just don't know it yet, so we play small. We play depressed. We play not-good-enough.

Now, right this second, tell the Universe: "Okay. I'm ready. Show me."

The Way to Zero

Zero Frequency® is not a destination. It is an approach to living, and you will get better at it over time. In this book, I have organized six main principles of Zero Frequency® that, when practiced consistently, will help you get to Zero and experience the bounty and freedom that is your birthright. This book is designed to be a field guide to Zero Frequency®, a tool you return to again and again as you grow in this discipline. So, please don't expect to "get to Zero" by the end of the book. Again, this is not about goals or a specific destination; this is a way of life—*the easiest way*—and it takes practice!

The next two chapters are designed to awaken you to the truth about yourself and the science of the mind. In Chapters 4 through 10, you will find different practices to live more at peace, at Zero Frequency®. As you know, practice makes perfect. Pick the ones that resonate with you and practice, practice, practice.

* *Chapter 4: Practice Responsibility*—You have the power to change anything about your life, including anything about yourself. To do that, you must take one hundred and one percent responsibility for everything in your life.
* *Chapter 5: Practice Innocence*—To free yourself from the perceived limitations you were conditioned to believe, you must start thinking like a child again and open yourself to the magic and joy of life!
* *Chapter 6: Practice Taking Leaps of Faith*—Having the courage to take risks and let Divinity guide us is the ultimate act of self-trust and one of the most important ingredients for success.

- *Chapter 7: Practice Gratitude*—When you practice gratitude, no matter what your circumstances, you raise your vibration to Zero Frequency® and connect to Zero, the field of all possibilities.

- *Chapter 8: Practice Letting Go*—Nature is effortless; it is always in flow and abundant. We, too, can experience this state, if we let go of control and allow the Universe to lead.

- *Chapter 9: Practice Peace*—When we have peace in our minds, we have peace in our lives. And when we have peace in our lives, there is more peace in the lives of those around us. This is how we co-create a peaceful world.

- *Chapter 10: Practice Abundance*—The ability to be happy and at peace for no reason is living in true abundance. This state opens doors, brings opportunities and ensures you always have what you need when you need it..

Please remember, getting to Zero is the goal; concentrate on the process and not the outcome. It is the easiest way to happiness and abundance. As you free your mind and remember who you really are, there is no need to set goals, or plan or figure out how to clear "obstacles" on your path. It is important that you start going around the obstacles. All is within you, and all is possible *for you*.

As you turn the page, thank you for keeping an open mind. I appreciate that you are here.

Chapter 2

Zero Frequency®: The Journey Back to Yourself

Our lesson is to learn to be. The freedom of being will extricate you from the oppression of doing. Herein lays the seed of knowingness that has the capacity to take you beyond all of this world's knowledge.
Eric Pearl

Think back to a time when you allowed yourself to simply be you, trusting yourself and the goodness of the Universe. Try to recall a moment when you followed your heart and made decisions based on your natural sense of knowing, believing that your choices were right even though you couldn't explain why. When you felt this way, you were living in the state of Zero Frequency®. And you were truly, authentically yourself.

What brought you to this book? A feeling that there is more to life, perhaps? A sense that you have so much more to experience, to give, to love? A desire to step into the life you know is waiting for you, if only you could find the way? Do you see? You already know that you are not being yourself. Though you may not have had the words to describe this feeling, you yearn to get back to Zero, back to yourself.

You may *think* you are being yourself, but most of the time you are not. This is true for all of us. We are all conditioned to be concerned with the opinions of others, constantly seeking their approval, changing like chameleons based on what we believe they expect of us. So great is our fear of rejection that the vast majority of us are willing to become whomever we feel others need us to be in order to be accepted, instead of trusting in our own being in the truth of who we are and what feels right in our hearts. Even when we are alone, we are uncomfortable with being ourselves. Our memories constantly take us back to those times when others have made us feel inadequate, when we felt rejected because we didn't act, speak or behave the way they wanted us to.

You are not those replayed memories. Whenever you allow your memories to control you, you are letting your subconscious mind make your choices and decisions for you. These memories take over your thoughts and feelings. They run your life. You think you are in control, but you are not.

Even when you gain approval from the outside world, even when others are pleased and happy with you, the feeling of satisfaction is only temporary, since those old worn-out and destructive programs and memories are replaying at the back of your mind. When the fleeting sense of satisfaction dissipates, you are left with the sense of emptiness. This emptiness is rooted in our betrayal of our own true selves. Is this the way you want to live? Really?

What matters most is what you think of yourself. You must love and accept yourself exactly the way you are—always. When you are okay, everyone else is okay with you. When you approve of and love yourself, others love you and approve of you too. That is the way we all came into this world, and that is the way we all truly wish to live in our hearts.

There have probably been times when you didn't care what others thought. You were so sure and confident in yourself and felt so good and strong in your heart that you didn't worry what anyone said or thought. Then and only then did you discover the truth of your heart: that you were invincible and that everything was possible. See, when you are yourself, you know the sky is the limit. You embrace a powerful Universal Law. You know beyond the shadow of a doubt the ultimate truth: that we are all limitless beings.

When you are truly yourself, you feel happy for no reason. You feel good in your own skin. You don't depend on being approved or accepted. You are okay being different. You don't have a problem with making a fool of yourself in front of people. You feel content and at peace no matter what goes on around you. At Zero, you are *you*, so you feel content, complete, and happy in your heart. You know you can conquer the world. You understand that no one can stop you. You become certain again that everything is possible. What others think ceases to be important. It is the state of being in bliss, pure and simple.

This is Zero Frequency®, and this can be you.

What Keeps You Off Zero?

In his book, *The Untethered Soul,* Michael Singer explains the difference between self and what he calls "personal self." He writes, "Your self is the pure stream of consciousness, that just keeps on flowing. Your personal self is the identity you form, based on how your inner voice perceives this stream of consciousness and the thought patterns that emerge from it."

In other words, you are not your thoughts. You are also not your feelings, or your memories or your limiting beliefs. Your thoughts, feelings, memories and beliefs are simply replaying over and over again, and you hear them. When you pay attention to them, when you act on them as if they are telling you the truth, as if this is who you are, you instantly leave Zero Frequency®. The old memories and programs that play and replay in your mind will get you off balance—and keep you there. This is important to realize because you are the only one who can stop them from playing and bring yourself back to Zero.

Singer goes on to write, "Once you realize there's a difference (between self and personal self), you'll look at yourself in a whole different light. The path of letting go allows you to free your energies so that you can free yourself."

So what are some of the thoughts that keep you from being yourself? I wish to soothe your intellect. In truth, we are all created perfect; we *are* all created as unique beings. The "imperfections" are mistaken judgments, opinions, beliefs we have accumulated and memories and programs—many of them ancient—some that we "inherited" from our ancestors.

You must let go of everything that is not you. You must erase the memories in your subconscious mind that are controlling your life and allow yourself to be guided by a more intelligent part of you—your superconscious mind. Being who you really are means letting go and letting God erase all your programs, all your old preconceptions and painful memories. There is nothing out there; all is inside you. This is why I always tell people: "I found the easiest way to do it! You let go and give God permission to erase. You don't even have to dig up, nor think about, nor understand what memories are the ones causing you problems. This process does not require remembering painful or triggering experiences. It is as simple as letting go and allowing God, Divinity or the Universe—whatever name you want to give this divine force—to erase what is no longer useful to you.

When you erase the memories and programs that have shaped your world, you also help free others from those memories and programs. Let me give you an example I sometimes use in my live seminars to demonstrate this. I write a problem on a chalkboard and I ask the participants, "Can you see the problem?"

Everyone says, "Yes."

Then I erase the problem, and I ask them, "Can you see it now?"

They say, "No."

Then I write another problem, but this time I invite someone from the audience to erase it. We do this a couple of times with different people coming to the stage to erase. And then I ask them: "What is this telling you? Any idea?"

Well, no matter who erases it from the board, the problem is erased for everyone. Just as in this metaphoric example, the memories that get erased in you get also erased in your family, your relatives and ancestors. You are even erasing it from generations to come because we all hold common memories; this is the reason we show up in each other lives.

Most everything you have decided to believe about yourself is false and does not define you in any way. Now, "erasing" does not mean forgetting. No, we do not fall into a state of amnesia in which we don't remember. What we let go of, what gets erased, are the pain and judgments associated with and created by these memories. We can remember and observe them, but we are free of the triggering negative effect they have on our lives and we no longer have the need to react.

You are not your problems, your opinions, or your judgments. You are above all that. You are a Universal being having an earthly experience. That Universe is in you; it is *the part of you that knows best;* it is who you really are! This is very important to acknowledge and live by on your path to happiness, peace, wealth and success.

At first, staying at Zero—staying conscious—may last only briefly. Making this happen takes discipline and practice. You are learning to re-educate your mind. And, as the Zen saying goes, the mind is restless like a monkey. In the present—at Zero—you have everything you need at your fingertips. You are at one with the whole cosmos and can observe instead of engage. Please know, as soon as you ask yourself, or think, "Am I at Zero?" you are not. At Zero Frequency®, there is no thinking, no questioning and no ego.

On cloudy days, we forget that the sun is still shining above the clouds. We look for the breaks, those moments when the clouds part and we can see the clear blue sky. Our memories and programs are just like those clouds, making up stories, constantly nagging at us and getting in our faces, lamenting and regretting the past or worrying about the future. When you are yourself, back at Zero, you are once again living in the present. You have created a break in the clouds, allowing the sunshine back in.

Your only job is to become your true self again; you must remember how to simply *be*. You must let go of all the knowledge and beliefs in your mind, unlearn everything you have taught yourself, so you can reconnect with your own wisdom, your true self, the wisdom of your heart.

When you simply be, you are in your natural and unique rhythm, and that is when you connect with the rhythm of Divinity. You are one with the Universe. You are in that flow that takes you to the right place at the right time, with the right people, effortlessly. You are at Zero Frequency®.

When Everything Is Right and Perfect

Now is the time to realize that being yourself is the key to everything that is right and perfect for you. You do not and cannot know what this is. The way to find out is to return yourself to Zero and give permission to *the part in you that knows* to show you. This does not mean you will live a life without problems. Many believe the correct definition of happiness is a life without problems. However, that is not true. Life is and will always be about problems because without challenges, there would be no opportunities for us to grow. Life would be so boring without problems! We are here to evolve, to change and grow. We are here to learn from our experiences, to find the blessings behind every challenge and to rediscover our true identity.

The only way for us to do this is to let go and let God. We must give permission to the part in us that created us and that knows better than anyone else does, what is right for us. The Universe is simply waiting for us. So wake up, open the door and let go, so you can tune back into Zero Frequency® and return to being your true self.

My own life changed dramatically once I began making the journey back to myself. I felt free for the first time in my life, accepting the truth that I am one hundred percent responsible for everything that happens in my own experience. Before that, like all of us, I was hopelessly at sea creating my own messy reality, and I didn't even know it. Like you, I tried to convince myself that I was in control, while the truth was exactly the opposite.

When I met my teacher, I woke up and began the journey back to myself, discovering that my happiness and my freedom did not depend upon anyone or anything outside myself. When this happened, I began to feel lighter, happier and more content than I had believed possible. I realized I didn't need to be perfect. That was a big one for me, always trying to be the perfect mother and wife or, even worse, the perfect accountant! Talk about impossible!

None of us is perfect, not in the sense that we understand the idea. We are all utterly unique. Each one of us is born with our own gifts and talents, and with a purpose no one else on earth came here to fulfill. No one else on this planet can do what you can do, precisely the way you do it. Please know there is a part in you that is perfect and that knows everything. You are a special child of God.

When I realized I was okay just the way I was and didn't need to be perfect in the eyes of the world, I went to the partners at the CPA office where I was working and told them I would not be doing tax research for them anymore. They were surprised and asked why, telling me I had done amazing work in the past.

I explained that, although I could do it, tax research was not one of my unique talents, and surely there were others in the office, naturally good at precisely that job, who would probably be far more expeditious than I was. I also pointed out that the company would make more money using them instead of me. You see, I was best at preparing taxes, accounting, and meeting a deadline. I could also solve problems and accomplish more in less time than others could. However, when it came to tax research, others were far better than I was.

We each have our unique talents and are naturally gifted in certain areas where we can surpass others. It's good to recognize this. When I got back to being myself, my unique gifts became crystal clear to me.

Many years ago I took a seminar where I was asked the question, "What would you be doing, even if you were not paid to do it, because you loved it and it gave you satisfaction?" At the time, I was committed to my work of accounting and tax preparation. But I wasn't truly happy. I wasn't living my passion. I answered, "I would travel the world sharing with others what has helped me."

Definitely there is a part in us that knows. As I shared earlier, some years later I left my accounting practice to do exactly that. I was finally trusting and living my soul's purpose. All the self-help trainings I had taken, I had taken for myself, for my own growth. I never took any training with the thought that I wanted to teach or even change careers. I just started promoting and organizing for teachers whose training had made a profound difference in my life.

Then one day, I stumbled upon my passion, the path that was right and perfect for me. My teacher told me that he was going to retire. By that time, I was assisting him, even teaching "officially" alongside him. We were coming back from giving a training, and he said, "Please remove my photo from the flyers; I am not going to teach anymore."

That was the first time it occurred to me, "Maybe I can do this."

Up to that time, teaching had been just a hobby, part of my weekend activities. I asked him to meditate and ask inwardly if teaching was the right thing for me to do. He did that and got an okay. Then he added, "You just need to be yourself. No need to study or get a title."

I learned early on in this new career of mine how right my teacher had been. When I worried about preparing to give talks, he told me to trust myself and speak from the heart. He explained that I would lose my spontaneity if I planned what I would say. When I let go and allowed the words to flow, knowing I was being my pure self in the moment, the right and perfect words *for that moment* and *for that audience* came to me.

Begin by remembering that you don't need to do anything other than be yourself. You don't owe your loyalty to anything or anyone who limits the expression of your soul. You don't depend on others' acceptance. Relax. Once you are at Zero Frequency® you will see that you feel right at home. Rewards will multiply and miracles will simply happen. All of this will come to you without effort. Spread your wings and fly!

Listen to Your Heart...
This Is Where the Wisdom Is

When we lose our magic, we fall back on placing the intellect above the heart, which is what most of us have been conditioned to do. We lead what Henry David Thoreau called "lives of quiet desperation," filled with a sense of hollow emptiness. Zero Frequency® is where you return to the magical state of perfect awareness, bypassing the intellect, allowing Inspiration to flow back into your heart.

No matter how many degrees you may have or how smart you are, you will never reach that place of pure awareness with your intellect. Zero Frequency® is an experience that can be neither described nor explained in terms of logic. Your intellect will struggle to understand the simple concepts in this book, but to succeed, you must put your conscious mind aside and allow your heart to guide you. Zero Frequency® may speak to the intellect, but it is for the heart, teaching you how to free your soul and return to the source of all joy.

Zero Frequency® steers you in the direction of listening to your inner voice and Inspiration when solving problems rather than to your programming or to those memories that created all your problems in the first place. By learning how to consciously access your innate wisdom, you will be able to bring yourself back to Zero Frequency® every time your intellect tries to take you out of the present moment.

The secret is inside you. All you have to do is learn how to let go and reconnect with your essence. Your true identity is the key to your freedom. This freedom requires that you become more conscious and present, because when you become aware, the magic happens. At Zero Frequency® you will find that you have everything you need, that you have had it all along, that there is no right or wrong, and that you are now and have always been pure of heart. You will see the world as God sees it, accepting everything as perfect in this moment. You will experience peace beyond understanding.

You cannot be the servant of two masters. It's living from Inspiration at Zero Frequency® (Paradise) or from your programs (Hell). The choice is yours.

The Journey Begin...

In our state of unconsciousness, we are a million miles away from our true selves, unable to see that everything we need is right in front of us. We are never truly present, believing instead the voice of our intellect that tells us it knows better and, in so doing, obscuring from our awareness all other options and possibilities. Rigid intellectual expectations make us look in all the wrong places, ask all the wrong questions. We are taught that trusting our heart is a form of weakness, so we disregard the very voice we should be listening to, the voice of our Inspiration.

When you are at Zero, your intellect, emotions and the memories playing in your subconscious mind no longer dominate you. You are free. You become an open channel, receiving the right ideas and perfect solutions. In this place you begin to hear things you have never heard before. You become an observer, noticing things you have never seen before.

You are the only one who can begin the journey back to yourself by letting go of your toxic and destructive memories and programs. Yes, you can escape the judgments, opinions and beliefs you have created about and for yourself. In short, you can escape the tyranny of your own mind. And when you rid yourself of all that nonsense accumulated throughout your lifetimes, you will be back at Zero Frequency®, able to flourish and flow with all the goodness of God's Universe, effortlessly.

In the next chapter, I will explain how your mind works so you can finally let go of your self-judgment about your negative experiences, feelings and outcomes. Once you understand how your mind works and how you can get it to work for you, you will see that Zero Frequency® offers you the easiest path to happiness, abundance and peace.

Don't be afraid to be yourself. Returning to the truth of who you are is a practice and a discipline. And it is easier than you think. Once you start practicing, it becomes natural. It's like riding a bike again after years without it. It will all come back to you. You've simply forgotten who you really are. Now is the time to remember and begin the journey back to yourself—the journey back home.

Connect to ZERO *frequency*

1. When limiting thoughts or doubts take you to the past, they leave no room for you to be who you really are. An easy way to disengage from the stress this causes is to smile. Yes, really! A 2012 study[*] found that holding a smile—even a forced smile—will change your brain's chemistry, giving you both physiological and psychological benefits.

2. Set aside your self-judgment and become the observer. Remember, you are not those thoughts, feelings and reactions. This is especially important as you read this book and practice connecting to Zero Frequency®. When you are the observer, it is much easier to determine if your actions and reactions come from the past or come from who you really are. Are your feelings helping you return to self? What about your thoughts? Your habits? The simple act of noticing these things will help you break free from that which is not authentically you. You can repeat mentally: "I let go and trust."

---

[*] "Grin and Bear It: The Influence of Manipulated Facial Expression on the Stress Response," Tara L. Kraft, Sara D. Pressman (Psychological Science, Volume 23, Issue 11, 2012).

3. I mentioned Michael Singer's wonderful book, *The Untethered Soul.* Here is an excerpt for you to consider: "(Blind) People who walk with the use of a cane often tap (it) from side to side. They're not trying to find where they should walk; they are trying to find where they *shouldn't* walk. They're finding the extremes." When we are in Zero Frequency®, we are in balance. We are walking down the center of the path, steering clear of the edges (extremes). Be mindful—are you walking near an edge, or are you balanced in the center?

4. Give yourself the gift to be your authentic self in front of everybody. Remember, when you are at Zero Frequency®, you are in flow and your natural rhythm connects with the rhythm of the Universe. No need to be afraid to be yourself in front of others; you don't depend on their approval to be happy. Show them with your example that they can also be *their* authentic selves.

You can find more resources on how to go back to Zero Frequency® at *www.zerofrequency.com/bookresources*

Chapter 3

How Your Mind Really Works

*Even if a man conquers thousands of men on the
battlefield, only he who conquers himself
will win his battle.*
Teaching of the Buddha

I f right now you're wondering, "How can being happy and living in peace and abundance be as easy as Mabel claims?" I understand. You're a seeker and you've put a lot of effort into creating a new life. Perhaps, like so many of my students, you have spent countless hours trying to convince yourself to think positively. Maybe you've tried to control your thoughts, written pages of affirmations, and tried to visualize a specific outcome, only to end up disappointed.

Or perhaps you have simply been trying to solve your problems through willfulness. You implement new strategies in an effort to improve your financial situation. Maybe you try a new diet in your tenth attempt to lose weight. Perhaps you drastically change your appearance in order to attract a partner. If you were rewarded with some fruits from your labor, but you still felt unhappy and unsatisfied, you may have started to feel as though it was your own fault. "I just have to write *more* affirmations," you told yourself. *Do better. Try harder.*

It's not your fault. It's simply the way you were programmed, the way your mind works.

We are not our bodies or our minds. We have three parts: The superconscious, which is your spiritual side; the conscious, which is your intellect; and the subconscious (your inner child), which, like a computer, stores your memories and emotions. While your conscious mind is aware of some of your memories, others are buried deep in your subconscious mind. Your life circumstances and experiences are the true reflections of memories, actions, deeds and thoughts from the past that are triggered and activated by current situations and people. Can you see how relying on your conscious mind is limiting?

Now consider working with affirmations and visualizations in order to attract a better life. The Law of Attraction postulates that these tools will help us create the reality we desire. Based on the way most understand this law, if you want a new house, you are advised to visualize how the house looks and how you feel walking through its rooms, turning on the chimney, leisurely relaxing in the backyard and so on. The instruction is to feel yourself in your desired reality as if it has already happened and, in so doing, give it the energy that allows it to manifest.

In his book, *The User Illusion: Cutting Consciousness Down to Size,* Tor Norretranders explained that the conscious mind only uses sixteen bits of information per second, while eleven million bits of information—memories, experiences and thoughts from the past—are playing and replaying in your subconscious mind, interfering with them. Visualization and positive thinking activate only the sixteen bits, the part of you that believes it knows what is right for you and, therefore, gives orders to God, treats God as a servant, and tells God when and where to show up and what to do.

However, your conscious mind *doesn't know* what is right and perfect for you in every moment; among the millions of bits of information outside of your consciousness are the limiting programs, and they, too, are talking to you. Sometimes the volume is so low that you don't hear what they're saying, but they generate a power of attraction all the same. Thoughts such as:

- "I'm not good enough."
- "I don't have a good education."
- "I don't deserve it."
- "Life is hard."
- "I don't have enough money."
- "Life is unfair."

What type of reality do you think these thoughts will attract? What decisions will they unconsciously lead you to make? They will create an opposite force greater than your positive intentions. Worse, trying to use your conscious, limited mind to manifest can cause disappointment, temporary remedies or unwanted consequences. In her article titled, "Why Positive Affirmations Don't Work,",* Dr. Sophie Henshaw states, "The reason positive affirmations don't work is that they target the conscious level of your mind, but not the unconscious. If what you are trying to affirm

---

* https://psychcentral.com/blog/why-positive-affirmations-dont-work/

is incongruent with a deeply held negative belief, then all that results are inner struggles."

Einstein said, "We cannot solve our problems with the same thinking we used when we created them." We try to solve problems with our intellects—through positive thinking, or other outward changes—but they are not there. *Your problems are not in your body, your external world or even in your mind.*

Your power does not come from the conscious mind but from the connection you have with the Universe. The library of the Universe is within you. Your authentic wisdom resides in the heart. You know everything, but you don't know it consciously. When you use visualizations and affirmations, you're using only that small part that thinks it knows, but, in reality, it doesn't know. It doesn't know if a particular house is the right one for you or how much money you actually need to be at peace and happy. And the memories in your subconscious mind might be counteracting the conscious desires.

We need a system, an art, by which our subconscious and superconscious work together. Ho'oponopono, a spiritual path created by Hawaiians and practiced by people around the world, is this art. It goes beyond the Law of Attraction. Ho'oponopono engages all those eleven million bits of information per second without you knowing or needing to know and understand exactly how. All you need to do is let go and allow the *part in you that knows* more than you do, to release any limiting programs and to make the corrections.

In this chapter, I will share more about your subconscious and superconscious mind and offer you simple techniques to disrupt the negative patterns.

The Perfection of Your Superconscious Mind

The spiritual side of you, the part of you that no matter what is happening within you or outside of you, is always perfect and at peace, this is your superconscious mind. It's the part that *knows* and, above all, is very clear on who it is all the time. Your superconscious is always connected to God and has access to universal wisdom. Simply put, your superconscious knows better. It also understands that everything is perfect.

God is your source of Inspiration and communicates with you through your superconscious. When you are called to help others; when you are overcome with a desire to create something; when you feel the pull of a different city, job or even a brand-new life, that is your Inspiration. Most people don't answer the call or create the thing, or follow their yearning for something new. Why? Because they don't trust it. They want to assess their Inspiration with the conscious mind, but you can't apply logic to the divine. It just is. And it is perfect.

The Power of Your Subconscious Mind

While your conscious mind is your intellect and your superconscious mind is your spiritual side, your subconscious mind is your physical and emotional side. Even though you are not aware of it, your subconscious is responsible for what you manifest in your life. We believe we are living consciously, but we are really living in the subconscious mind.

This part of you stores all of your memories and is your inner child, your computer bank. Drawing on past experiences and thoughts, this is the part of you that suffers, that lives in fear, that tells yourself you can't do whatever you wish to do or have whatever you wish to have. Your intuition also comes from your subconscious and alerts you to potential problems or dangers. Your subconscious also runs your body. Your digestive system digests and your heart pumps without you having to think about it or direct it to do so. The emotions you experience and the way you react in any given situation come from a memory stored in your subconscious that starts playing automatically, just as your heart pumps automatically.

So, when you try to think your way out of something or tell yourself to change or react differently, your subconscious mind sometimes has a different agenda. If you've ever wondered, "Why can't I figure this out?" or, "Why am I still stuck?" it's likely that you are trying to solve something or attract something with your conscious mind and your subconscious has other ideas.

Everything in your tangible world—your relationships, your job, your home and possessions, your health—is a reflection of your inner world. This is good news! It means that you can learn to work *with* your subconscious, not *against* it. Your subconscious is powerful, and, when you pay attention to it and actively work to heal past experiences, you can harness that power to make even seemingly harrowing tasks seem easy. Dr. Hew Len, my teacher, used to say, "If you are looking for your best partner, this is it. Your inner child (subconscious mind)." Your subconscious can cooperate to find the right path to success with the fewest obstacles. You can answer the call of your superconscious mind and act on your inspiration. And in doing so, you welcome infinite possibilities.

The Reality of Your Conscious Mind

The only job of the intellect is to choose. It is the only part of us that has free choice. The intellect will choose to let go or not let go. The Ho'oponopono cleaning starts in the intellect, when you choose to say, "thank you," or use other tools or techniques to help you let go. Your conscious mind decides to let go of the memories that are rooted in your past, and that is an order that goes to the subconscious. Then the subconscious makes a connection with the superconscious.

In his seminar, "Unlock the Power of Your Mind," scientist, lecturer and author of *You Are the Placebo: Making Your Mind Matter,* Joe Dispenza, DC explains, "In order for us to truly change, we have to get beyond ourselves. That is one of the arts of transformation. The moment we are truly present, we cannot be running a program. When we are truly present, and we take our attention off our body, off of people in our lives, off of things, and places, and even time, that is the moment we become pure consciousness. That is the moment we are no longer playing by the laws by Newtonian physics…The moment we become nobody, no one, no thing, nowhere, no time, that's the moment we get beyond ourselves. That's the moment that allows us to see new possibilities that we could never see from the place where we are stuck in our own programs and personality."

Finding Your Three-Part Harmony

Now that you are aware of the three parts of you—the conscious, the subconscious and the superconscious—you can choose to work with them in harmony to help you create the life you desire.

The superconscious is the part of us that is always connected to God, no matter what is happening. It never interferes with the relationship between the intellect and the subconscious mind, which is like the relationship between mother and child, because it knows that everything is perfect.

Once permission is given to act, to erase, that's when Inspiration comes. And it comes through what Hawaiians call mana or divine energy. The intellect chooses to clean. The subconscious makes the connection to the superconscious. The superconscious connects to God. God erases, creates an empty space; then Inspiration comes. Once a memory is erased from the subconscious mind, it is then erased from the physical.

The subconscious is important because, besides being the part of your mind that manifests people, experiences, and things in your life, it facilitates the connection to Source. The conscious mind cannot go directly to Source; it needs the subconscious to make the connection to your superconscious mind when it decides to let go.

Maybe this is an easier way to understand the concept. Imagine you are a computer. You have a conscious (hardware) and a subconscious (software). You have a delete key and, when you press the delete key, you send instructions to your superconscious that you are choosing to let go. You don't have to understand how the computer works. You don't have to see the cables and how they connect. It just works. The same is true of you. You don't have to understand how it works or see how everything is connected. *You* just work.

When you work only on changing the physical, it's like putting a Band-Aid on the problem. If you really want to solve the problem, you need to work on your subconscious mind. What is the memory playing that is creating your physical world? It's not about how others treat you or hold you back. It's about you. As you change, everything changes, not the other way around.

Communicating with Your Inner Child

In Ho'oponopono, your subconscious mind is your inner child. It probably comes as no surprise to you to learn that your inner child is constantly neglected. Of course it is! Up until now, you may not have even known it existed. Or perhaps you had a vague idea of what it meant to have an inner child but had no idea how that role played out in your life. Now you know and now you can give your inner child the attention and love it needs.

Imagine your inner child is all of the memories of experiences you have not yet resolved. You may think you have moved past a troubling event simply because you grew up and stopped thinking about it, but your inner child knows better. Until you give your inner child the attention it desires and help your inner child heal those memories, it will continue to influence your outer world. Many of the undesirable experiences you have are direct results of ignoring your inner child. If you choose to communicate with your inner child, to love it and take good care of it and, eventually, let the memories go, you will easily harness the power of your subconscious mind to tap into the superconscious mind and live your life from Inspiration—life you are not even capable of imagining at this moment.

I understand if you think all of this talk of your inner child is a little bit "out there." When I first started on my spiritual path, I felt the same. Though my intellect told me it was silly, I decided to consider it. For example, if I felt worried or anxious, I would tell my inner child, "I love you. Everything will be okay. We are together now. We don't have anything to worry about." If I was afraid of an outcome, I would tell her, "This one we give to God directly. We don't even try." Even though I still doubted it would work, it calmed me down to talk to my inner child. Simply by acknowledging and reassuring my inner child, I began to feel peace in stressful situations.

You see, your inner child knows God; the intellect doesn't. This is why, when you tell your child, "Let's give this problem to God," it relaxes!

When I was teaching in Argentina, I met a fifteen-year-old autistic girl named Lucia. I asked her how I could help my adult students to connect with their inner child. Lucia told me, "That's easy, Mabel! You call her with love, and she comes. You call her by her name, and she comes."

Isn't that beautiful? *You call her with love, and she comes.* You call her by name, and she comes. Even though I knew she was speaking truth, experience told me that adults would have a hard time processing that advice. Then I said, "That's easy for you to say, Lucia, but I am talking to adults!"

Her grandmother, who had been listening to our conversation, decided to give Lucia's advice a try. It worked! She was able to connect to her inner child. So, while you're trying to understand this now, if you are feeling confused about *how* to connect to your inner child, please let go and surrender. It could be easier than you think.

Over time, this practice provided solutions to me from unexpected places. One day, at the supermarket, I was thinking about my weight. I had been on different diets for over a month and yet, every morning I'd get on the scale and the numbers were the same. I decided to have a conversation with my inner child. I asked her, "What is it that we don't want to let go of? Because no matter what I do, nothing works."

The answer came to me with the following thought: "Vanilla ice cream."

Immediately, I said to my inner child, "Of course, after we lose the weight, we are going to have a lot of vanilla ice cream, but first we need to lose the weight!"

At that point I heard my inner child say, "First, give me the vanilla ice cream, and then I'll help you. I'll cooperate."

Maybe I was going nuts, but at that moment I decided to show my inner child that I trusted her. So, instead of buying the gallon of vanilla ice cream at the supermarket, I went straight to the ice cream parlor and asked for a big vanilla ice cream cone. I actually took the time to eat it there. I enjoyed it, taking it as an outing, a fun activity with my inner child. The next morning, to my surprise, when I stood on my scale, I had lost two pounds!

I share this story because I want you to realize that when you ask how to let go, how to delete old memories, and you hear something ridiculous, you should do it anyway! You heard correctly. Always trust your own Inspiration.

Inspiration vs. Ego

True knowing comes from Inspiration. But how do you know, when making a choice and trying to be true to yourself, if you are coming from your programming (ego) or from Inspiration? You know by trusting what feels right in your heart, not your intellect. The secret is to act without thinking. That is Inspiration. For example, if a snake crosses your path, do you jump or do you think? If you think, you won't jump in time.

The snake will bite you before you make your decision. And this you know for sure: You don't want the snake to bite you!

This works for everything in life. When you do things naturally and instinctively, things just flow, and you later realize they were the perfect things to do. If, instead, you stop and ponder your options, analyzing them over and over again, you lose your natural rhythm. You stop being yourself, and everything becomes difficult. This happens because as soon as you begin to think and to worry, you are not in the flow. You are not at Zero, so Inspiration cannot come through. You can always choose which part of your mind you want to empower—the one that makes life difficult or the one that makes life easy.

Inspiration vs. Intuition and Dreams

Dr. Hew Len explained Inspiration to me in this way: "Inspiration always comes from God/Universe. It is an original idea or new information. It is usually the best solution or that perfect answer that cannot be explained." He also made it clear that Inspiration must not be confused with intuition. Intuition is part of our replayed memories, emerging from our subconscious mind. It is a recall of something that already happened in the past, and it comes from a part in you (the Inner Child) as a warning that it is going to happen again, so you can avoid it.

Inspiration, on the other hand, is always new, always in the present. It does not come from a past experience. It is like fresh air, closer to you than your own breath, renewed with every breath, and available twenty-four/seven. Inspiration is free, but most of us don't choose to use it.

Dreams, too, are replayed memories. Dreams can be premonitory or replays from prior experiences. No matter the case, they are opportunities to correct and let go, and you don't even need to understand them. Do you see why we say in Zero Frequency® that we need to let go twenty-four hours a day? You can actually prevent things from happening because you worked on them during a dream. But don't be surprised if Inspiration shows up in your dreams too. Some people find answers, innovative ideas and solutions to their problems in their dream states.

Inspiration can only come when we connect with the Universe with an open heart and without filters. Inspiration shows up as spontaneous ideas that seem to come out of nowhere. They come out of thin air.

They might not even make sense in the moment, but they'll turn out to be the perfect solutions you would never have thought of. I have had several significant experiences of this sort, and every time I trusted the uncertain, the unknown and the unexplainable, the results were amazing. I learned to trust and follow my heart (Inspiration), rather than my intellect (ego). What my intellect was telling me made every bit of common sense. However, what my heart was telling me was to trust, let go and go for it.

In my personal life, as I shared in the first chapter of the book, I made decisions that were illogical to the ego, but that followed the Inspiration of my heart. I left a marriage and a secure accounting job to start my own private accounting practice, which became a success. Later, I left behind this successful and secure life I had built for myself to begin my path as a spiritual teacher, conducting seminars and writing books that awaken people worldwide. At each step of the way I let go, trusted and tapped into Inspiration.

Left Brain vs. Right Brain

In 1996, Dr. Jill Bolte Taylor, a Harvard-trained scientist and published neuroanatomist, suffered a massive stroke in the left hemisphere of her brain.

Suddenly, this accomplished woman, who had built a life around using her brain, could not walk, talk or remember any of her life. It would take Dr. Bolte Taylor eight years to regain all of her physical and thinking abilities.

In her book, *My Stroke of Insight,* she refers to her left brain as her "story-teller." She said, "As my left brain language centers recovered and became functional again, I spent a lot of time observing how my storyteller would draw conclusions based upon minimal information. For the longest time, I found these antics of my storyteller rather comical. Until I realized that my left brain mind, full-heartedly expected the rest of my brain to believe the stories it was making up! We should always remember there are enormous gaps between what we know and what we think we know. I learned I need to be very wary of my story-teller's potential for stirring up drama and trauma."

According to The Heartmath Institute in San Jose, California, the brain is not only sending messages to the heart; the heart is also sending messages back. This discovery originated with the work of John Lacey and Beatrice Lacey, researchers in the field of psychophysiology. The Laceys observed that the heart sends information to the brain that affects how we view the world and even our performance.

Your left-brain hemisphere creates all the stories, worries and fears that keep you from being present. This is why I call it "the drama queen." When your left brain starts to stir up drama and create these stories, bring yourself back to the present moment. Come back to Zero, where you can be in the flow of God's Universe, which will always put you in the right place, at the right time, with the right people.

As Dr. Jill Bolte Taylor shares with us in her book, "My right mind is open to new possibilities, and thinks out of the box. It is not limited by the rules and regulations established by the left mind that created that box. Consequently, my right mind is highly creative in its willingness to try something new."

Understanding how your left and right brain works will help you as you read this book and practice the techniques that will support you as you live a happier, more peaceful life. To come back to present, you can tell yourself, "This is just a story my left brain is telling me. I don't believe it." This is a simple and, yes, an easy way to get to Zero Frequency®.

Connet to ZERO *frequency*

Matthew David Hurtado talks about a transformational process he calls "allowing." He says, "Allowing is not a weak process where you submit and say, 'Okay, I surrender. You win.' You overthrow the mind and get the job done, once and for all." Therefore, when you surrender, you reach that allowing state of being, as Hurtado calls it.

So, how can you (temporarily) disconnect from your logical, conscious mind to access your subconscious mind? How can you enter, as Hurtado calls it, "the allowing state of being"? The easiest way is to cause a disruption that breaks your focus. Here are some suggestions that will require but a few seconds. Over time, you'll find these techniques will work naturally.

1. In this chapter, you learned that your brain is like a computer. When you notice a thought or worry, remember that it is just the monitor showing you a memory playing in your subconscious mind. Give your brain a command just as you would give your computer a command. Simply tell your brain: "delete" or "I press the delete key." You are choosing to let go, instead of reacting and

engaging. Don't allow your brain to direct you! It's just a memory playing.

2. Mentally talk to your Inner Child as though you were talking to a little child and assure the child you will not abandon it. "You're okay. We're in this together. Nothing to worry about." Find the words that suit your needs best. You can lovingly ask your child, "Please, let go."

3. Another way to stop getting stuck in negative thought patterns is to tell your brain kindly, "Enough. I am busy." This will help you get back to the present moment without engaging with these thoughts.

4. When you want to open your mind so that you can see a problem in a different way and change your emotions and perception about it, take a break. Move to a different location: go outside, sit in a different room of your house or place of work, whatever is the easiest for you in that moment. A few minutes will make a world of difference.

5. When we pay attention to Inspiration, it guides us back to Zero, back to our authentic selves. So often we ignore or forget this heart-centered guidance because we immediately are caught up in trying to decide if we should follow it. A good way to stay connected to Inspiration is to remove

yourself from the trappings of everyday life and go to a place that fills you with reverence. Perhaps that place is near water, or on a mountain or even in your backyard. Or maybe that place is in an art museum or a quiet chapel. Wherever your place is, that reverence for natural, artistic or spiritual beauty will help calm your mind so you can hear the voice of Inspiration.

6. Tapping into your Inspiration is easy—all you have to do is ask and pay attention to its guidance. A simple *thank you* and *I love you* will help you calm down your chattering mind and allow Inspiration to come. Yes, you have to give permission to Inspiration to come into your life. It doesn't invade your privacy, nor try to impose like the ego does.

You can find more resources on how to go back to Zero Frequency® at *www.zerofrequency.com/bookresources*

Chapter 4

Practice Responsibility

*If you want to be successful, you have to take
100 percent responsibility for everything that
you experience in your life.*
Jack Canfield

Once I attended a Ho'oponopono training in Philadelphia. It wasn't my first; I kept going back as much as I could to learn more from my teacher, because, every time I went, I became aware of something that I hadn't realized before—a new understanding.

At this particular event, my teacher talked about the importance of taking one hundred percent responsibility for everything in our lives. I had heard his wisdom several times before and, though I trusted him, I hadn't taken it in fully. I wasn't happy. I was a person who was always trying to change the people around me and I was never satisfied with what I had materially. I tried to make things happen "my way." I was right, and everyone else was wrong.

Then, suddenly, I understood. "Oh!" I thought. "If I created everything, and I am one hundred percent responsible, that means *I can change it."*

For the first time in my life, I felt free. My heart was truly happy because I realized that I had the power to change whatever I wanted to change about my life. I had spent so much time and energy trying to change others so that my life would look and feel the way I wanted it to look and feel, and yet it never worked. Why? Because you can't change anyone else and because it is much easier to change yourself. In trying to get everyone to fall in line with my way of doing things, I was making others responsible for my own happiness, prosperity, wellness and peace of mind. Do you see why I finally felt free? For the first time I understood the lesson: I am responsible, which means I can create and change at will. I recovered my power.

We tend to think of the word "responsibility" as a weighted word, as something we have to do. But really, in the context of our own lives, taking responsibility is a beautiful opportunity that yields immeasurable rewards. You see, when you blame people or complain about a situation that seems out of your hands, you give your power away. You depend on other people to resolve a problem, to make you feel better, to make you feel loved, to provide for you and so on. You cannot be truly happy when you depend on others in these ways.

Practice responsibility. It is the most important foundation of the Zero Frequency®, and without this, you will find it difficult to get to Zero. When you do practice taking one hundred percent responsibility, you will immediately come back to present, be more conscious and set yourself free.

What Does It Mean to Be One Hundred Percent Responsible?

Legend has it that, when the European conquerors' ships approached the shores of the Americas, the Native People could not see them, because they had no "program" in their minds that could read this information. "Reality"—what you see out there—is the result of your own perception and interpretation.

Taking one hundred percent responsibility means to see everything as an expression of something that is playing inside you. I know that you experience what is happening in your external life as very real, but the truth is, you create your own reality with your thoughts. You've probably heard this message before, but I am not referring to manifestation necessarily. I am referring to how your brain processes information. Your eyes only detect the information that your brain sends them. It is important to understand that not everyone sees the way you do. What you "see" is interpreted through your inner filters, which are conditioned by your old programming. In other words, you see (interpret) through your own memories and programs. In the last chapter, you learned that this is the function of your subconscious mind. Understanding how your mind processes information will help you become more patient and accepting of other peoples' points of view.

You are one hundred percent responsible for the way you interpret reality and the different situations you attract into your life. We are all familiar with the Law of Attraction. Now, you have to know that the reality you attract is not only determined by what you are aware of and think in your conscious mind. It is also the outcome and consequence of the memories you are holding in your subconscious mind that are constantly playing, creating and recreating "realities."

Most of the time, incidents occurring in a present moment are not caused by what is happening in that moment. They are caused by past actions, experiences you had during childhood, beliefs you've been holding onto and even decisions you could've made during your birth. Sometimes memories are obvious, and you can easily recognize them. They show up as your reactions, your beliefs, your opinions and judgments. Now you can choose *not* to buy into them, and *not* to engage with them. You can choose to think differently and adopt alternate attitudes. You have free choice. You're the only one who can let go of your limiting thoughts and beliefs.

Accepting one hundred percent responsibility does not mean that you are guilty of anything. Please don't confuse responsibility with guilt. Everything is a product of your own memories that repeat themselves, and you can choose to let go. Simply press the delete key instead of arguing with the monitor.

You can turn everything in your life around. You created your life, and you have the power inside of you to change it! Just as it took me a few trainings to fully understand what it meant to take one hundred percent responsibility, you may need to come back to this chapter more than once to remind yourself. Be patient with yourself as you process this. The truth will come.

Are You a Victim?

Nick Vujicic was born without arms and legs; he has one foot but no leg. Despite these challenges, Nick handles most of his daily chores on his own. He dresses and cleans himself, cooks, goes up and down the stairs, types forty-three words per minute on the computer and even swims in the pool! And he does all that while being in a great mood! You can watch him on YouTube. He has no arms, no legs and no problems! He gives motivational speeches, and I cannot think of anyone more qualified to do that than Nick.

If Nick is lacking anything, it's a victim's mentality. Why? Maybe the answer is in this quote by John W. Gardner, who was a United States Secretary of Health, Education and Welfare: "Self-pity is without a doubt the most destructive of the non-pharmaceutical narcotics; it is addictive, gives temporary pleasure and separates the victim from reality."

In Zero Frequency® we say that self-pity is an addiction, a memory replaying. It's been playing and replaying in our mind for so long that it has become so natural to us that it's hard to let go of. These kinds of thoughts keep playing and playing in our mind: "I can't do it... I don't have what it takes... I don't deserve it... I am not as good as..."

Consciously, we don't think that we get any benefit or payoff from seeing ourselves as victims, but that's not true. We will never admit it, but as a "victim," we might get more attention and care. Maybe someone will provide for us and we will not need to make an effort or get out of our comfort zone.

While giving a Ho'oponopono training in Romania, I met two sisters. After the end of the first day, they came to the front of the room to talk to me. I had not noticed them during the training; they had been sitting in the back of the room.

One of the women seemed very agitated. I'll call her Katja. She explained that she was very angry because she had come to the training expecting me to cure her sister of her mental disability. I looked over at her sister—I'll call her Sylvie—and that's when I noticed that she was somewhere else; that she wasn't connecting with reality.

I spoke with Katja for about thirty minutes reinforcing what she'd learned that day about letting go of expectations, about trusting God and so on. She was still upset with me because she wanted her sister to be "normal."

Then I said, "You want your sister to be like you? Is that it? You want her to be angry and upset because that is 'normal' for you. When I look at your sister, I see that she is okay. She is happy. She doesn't really have a problem—*you* have a problem with her."

Still upset with me, Katja left with her sister. I did not expect them to come back the next day, but they did.

The second day of our event was very interactive. This time, I noticed the sisters right away. In fact, Sylvie seemed like a different person. She was engaged and participated in all of the exercises. Katja, too, seemed different. She was smiling and hugging people. And, at the end of the class, she joined everyone in the dancing. Watching her, I could tell that she felt free. Throughout the day, I kept thinking, *what is going on?* What changed?

After the class, I found the sisters and I asked Katja what was different.

"I had a revelation last night," she explained. "I suddenly knew that Sylvie's mental disability had been meant for me, but her soul chose to take it on so that I would not have to."

Now, this may be true or not, but Katja had a completely different attitude than she had had the day before, and she viewed the situation with her sister in a new light. She no longer saw herself as a victim, *and* she no longer saw Sylvie as "not normal."

Whatever your situation, considering yourself a victim has no advantage. If you are a victim, you are powerless. Remember, depending on anyone or anything outside yourself will make you neither wealthy nor happy.

Do not fool yourself. Nothing good can come from being a victim. Maybe you will get attention but, in the end, it will play against you. So, if you find yourself "playing victim," think of all those people who have real limitations. Be grateful for everything you have and all the possibilities life offers you. Let go and choose to set yourself free from the addiction to victimhood. If you assume that you are the creator of your own reality, but at the same time you see yourself as a victim, you are giving your power away. In that moment, you are not the master of your destiny; you are at its mercy. You are at the mercy of others. You are choosing the great substitute for coping, which is comfort.

Things "Beyond Your Control"

It can be difficult to take one hundred percent responsibility when faced with painful, difficult, even tragic situations in our lives or the lives of the people around us. It is important to understand that it's not the tragedy itself, or what happened, or what someone did to you, that matters, but what you do with the decisions you make *about* what happened. You can choose to see yourself as a victim or you can learn from what happened. You can grow from what happened. You can become a better person and help others *because of what happened.*

Sometimes, a negative outcome is the way of closing a door so another one can open. Know in your heart that new opportunities will come. Focus on what you do and what *you* think, on the actions *you* take and the decisions *you* make; do not focus on those who "wronged" you. This is so important. Wish them well. If someone does you wrong, that is their problem, not yours. God sees everything, and everything comes back.

Most of the time we are asleep and we don't take responsibility for how we respond to a tragedy or a negative life event. And when we do this repeatedly, we end up in a prison of the mind. It's time to wake up and set yourself free!

Jamaican spiritual teacher Mooji shared these insights in a 2008 interview[*] «"I do not feel that this universe is revengeful, I feel it is corrective. It offers you countless opportunities so that you can, in some way, evolve. Even when it seems that we receive a punishment, it is actually an act of grace, although at first we do not know how to appreciate it. You often say thank you to the wrong person, the one that makes you feel sweet at the moment. You say thank you for the chocolate flavored moments. But some things bite, crunch and squeeze you, and you do not say thank you. But those things change your being in such a way that they bring wisdom to your experience."

Mooji went on to tell a story that had happened when he visited Spain. A man came to him and asked for a mantra. Mooji told him that he would give him a universal mantra, the best mantra, one that anyone can say. The mantra was *Thank you*. And he explained: "Just keep saying thank you. Do not explain, do not complain; just say thank you. Say thank you to existence. You do not have to justify it. Somehow, your being is cleansed and comes to life. Say thanks for all the beings that appear in your life. If you do not understand what they bring you, say thank you. If you are

* *Intensive Satsang with Mooji, part three, London, June 15, 2008, United Kingdom. Accessed August 31, 2018: https://youtu.be/g9Q14FbHw4A*

kicked, maybe you will not say thank you right away, but something inside of you, will. Say thank you and see what happens."

Thank you works miracles. It changes you and the people around you. Let me share an example. One of my students in Los Angeles told me that he had been robbed. His response was to say *Thank you* to the thief. When he did, the robber started giving him back everything he had taken and asked him, "Where do you live?" When my student told him where, the thief said, "That's not a safe neighborhood. Let me go with you." The thief acted as his bodyguard!

Some people find it unbelievable, and yet, this is only one story of many. I told this story at a seminar I gave in Paraguay. One of the participants told me something similar had happened to her. "I thanked the robber and tried to convince him to take my watch, which was very expensive," she told me. The robber refused, gave her back her things, and they ended up going out for coffee together!

When you let go, you are turning on a light and you are not only doing it for yourself. As you turn on the light for yourself, it gets turned on for everybody. The light does not discriminate. We live in a Universe where everything is connected! Let's say *Thank you* or *I love you* and let's spread more love, happiness and peace in the world. You can make a big difference in the world with a simple *Thank you.*

What Is Your Excuse?

Excuses are reasoned, justified fears that keep us stuck. If we listen to them, we give control to our fears and miss many opportunities. Typical excuses may be that we committed to something too difficult, or we don't have time or money, or we simply blame other people or circumstances for our inactivity. As with all memories, all we can do is press the delete key and let go.

Whenever you have an excuse, be aware that it's just a memory playing. Do not buy into it. Notice and stay present. Be confident. Trust. Go for it! When you say, "Okay, okay, I will do it tomorrow. I am not in the mood today," or, "I do not have time now," you procrastinate. These excuses will always be there. You have to commit. Many times we "fail" because we leave things for later. You decided to start that diet next Monday, didn't you? The worst part of not complying with the agreements we've made with ourselves is feeling bad, feeling like a failure and ending up doing nothing. We enter into a vicious circle, a spiral that takes us lower and lower until we hit bottom. Then we ask why our dreams still wait for us on the horizon.

Your dreams will only "come true one day" if you take responsibility. Commit to do what it takes. Reach for them. Work for them. Claim them as your own.

Connect to ZERO *frequency*

No matter what your circumstances are, be willing to take responsibility. Everybody who shows up in your life is giving you the chance to see the programs running in you that you are ready to release. As I shared in the story about my students befriending their robbers, we are all connected. What hurts one of us, hurts us all. And, what heals one of us, heals us all. So, by taking full responsibility for your life, you are not only freeing yourself from the prison of your own programs, but you are that freedom to all of us. Whatever is erased from you is erased from everybody, especially from your family, relatives and ancestors.

Here are a few simple ways to connect to Zero Frequency® through practicing responsibility:

1. When you accept responsibility, this does not mean that you are accepting *guilt*. I'm not suggesting you admit fault. To stay in the present, simply say, "I am sorry for whatever is in me that created this." With this simple phrase, you are letting go and giving permission for whatever is in you to be erased.

2. Stay conscious and become an observer. Do not take things personally. Connect with the power within you by saying, "It's just me. I created it. I can change it."

3. Override the voices and stories in your head by repeating mentally, "I let go and trust." Remind yourself, "It's just the program playing. It's just a movie."

4. Don't be afraid of fear and doubts. Repeat mentally: "Everything is perfect. Everything will be okay. This, too, shall pass."

You can find more resources on how to go back to Zero Frequency® at *www.zerofrequency.com/bookresources*

Chapter 5

Practice Innocence

If you want to be creative, stay in part a child, with
the creativity and invention that characterizes children
before they are deformed by adult society.
Jean Piaget

Remember when you were a child and had no worries, when you believed anything was possible? When you were young, a day lasted an eternity and life was full of magic and promise. You loved to sing, so you sang. You imagined a tree house, so you built it. You envisioned becoming a dancer, or a firefighter or a boat captain, and you believed you could easily step into that life. You knew that you could accomplish wonderful things—and you did.

When you were a child, your thoughts were limitless because you were living naturally at Zero Frequency®. Your connection to the Universe was pure and direct. You were free to be who you were. But then, as you grew older, you began to internalize other people's opinions, negative experiences and ideas, and your own painful experiences. Over time, you became conditioned to believe in your limitations. You stopped believing in yourself and lost your magic. You lost your passport to the state of Zero Frequency®.

By the time you were an adult, you silenced the voice of your intuition and inspiration so you could hear the "voice of reason." You didn't sing as much, plans for new tree houses were left unfinished and, even when you could catch a glimpse of the type of life you wanted to live, you now doubted your ability to get there. You let go of your dreams and shifted your focus from your heart to your head. Your mind became filled with concerns, fears and doubts, and you barely noticed as some of the color went out of your life. Perhaps you even stopped believing in happy endings.

You don't have to live this way. Your story can have a happy ending, and it can be as magical, wondrous and limitless as the endings you dreamed up as a child.

Children can be more insightful than adults can. We would be much happier if we practiced looking at the world the way a child sees it. In one of my presentations in Guadalajara, Mexico, two boys around eight years old came up to the stage during one of the breaks. One of the boys had drawn everything I had been talking about. The other one told me that he had a friend who was feeling lonely because his parents were not home much. He said, "I really want to help him. What can I tell him?"

I looked at him and said, "Tell him God is with him always and that is all he needs. He is never really alone." Then I asked him, "Do you think your friend will understand it?"

The boy replied, "Yes, for sure he will. I will tell him that."

Do you see? He did not question whether God is always with us. He did not doubt the possibility that his friend could feel better. He came to the stage with an innocent heart and trusted the wisdom he received.

After that exchange, I invited the two boys to stay on stage with me. A woman raised her hand and asked, "Mabel, they killed my husband, and I was there, and I cannot get this image out of my head."

Before I opened my mouth, one of the boys responded to her. "That is because you bring it to your mind and don't want to let go." We were all in awe. I didn't need to add anything else. Can you see? Children are much more ready to connect to Zero and stay in balance than we are. They are our teachers. They *know*. We need to start thinking as children do. We have much to learn from them.

It is my hope that, by now, you have begun to experience Zero Frequency®. In the last chapter, you learned about the power of practicing responsibility and that a simple decision made from your conscious mind can bring about immediate results. To accept responsibility is, in a way, an adult's job. Now, I am asking you to become a child again. Practicing innocence is a technique that will help you to quickly get to Zero Frequency®—and it will bring much joy to your life, because it's fun!

Free Yourself from the Need for the Material

As a child, I knew I could have everything I wanted and that I was not alone. I believed in God or a much greater power. I can't explain it in words; I was sure God existed. From a very early age I knew that everything was up to me and that life depended on our beliefs and our own efforts, that we are the creators of our own lives and are not victims of our circumstances.

I was the third girl in an emotional and close-knit family. New Year's Eve was always a big deal for us. At midnight, we would toast, and cry and kiss each other, so full of love and gratitude. When watching movies, every small thing would make us cry. At the same time, I was timid and had low self-esteem, and that stayed with me into adulthood.

When I married, my husband and I immigrated to the US. His family was more intellectual than mine, and they used to criticize us because we were too emotional for their taste. Because of my low self-esteem, I started thinking that there was something wrong with my family, that my in-laws were right, and we were wrong.

Influenced by their thinking, I bought into fear of the future and their desire for acquiring more of the best of everything. I entered the rollercoaster of the material world. We had a big house, but we were always saving to buy bigger and newer homes and nothing was ever enough. I became lost in the intellectual and material world; I bought into everybody's "not enough" syndrome and the need for material things to make me happy. The rat race never ended, because there was always something bigger and newer to buy. It was a constant source of anxiety.

Everywhere you go, people are not happy because they feel they are lacking something. They don't have enough money, enough recognition at work, enough possessions, enough of the "right" possessions. They are caught in "not enough" syndrome because they don't know themselves and they don't accept themselves. They base who they are—their self-worth, their identity and their purpose—on what they have.

I, too, had it backwards. I based my self-worth on my title and my possessions, and it is the other way around. When I finally woke up and started on my spiritual path, I started working on myself, reconnecting and remembering. As I became myself again, everything else came. Everything I could need or want was added.

Today, I live a very good life. I live in a nice place—a townhouse. I could afford something bigger, and the old me would have bought a very nice house, but I don't need it. So why would I buy a bigger house? To show people that I'm making money. I'm very happy in my townhouse. I love it and I'm grateful for it. So that is the difference. Before, I looked at material things to make me happy. Now, I simply enjoy them. I drive a nice car, but I don't have to spend all of my money on upgrading it. I don't need a bigger car; I enjoy the one I have.

When you are driven by a *need* to have more, and bigger and better things, that is an anxiety-producing state that makes it difficult for you to get to Zero Frequency®. Yet, to practice innocence, you don't have to give up your possessions. You simply must be aware of your neediness. In my Zero Frequency® trainings, I share a quote from Osho, who said, "If you lose everything, you will gain everything." I explain that this does not mean you have to give up your possessions to gain what you desire. In fact, Osho lived extravagantly and he enjoyed material things very much. He was not referring to material things; he meant you must lose your memories, programs and beliefs. The problem is not in having material things, but in putting them first.

The other thing we need to realize is that, when we leave, we take nothing with us. We say, "my house," and, "my car," but everything is borrowed. We leave this earth with nothing. Most of our lives we are thinking about the material possessions. How wonderful it is to realize that we don't have to concern ourselves with getting material things or owning them. We can simply enjoy them.

There is a saying that the richest person is not the person who has the most, but the person who needs the least. To be wealthy is to need less, because the riches are inside of you!

Free Yourself from Comparisons

We all do it: If you're like most people, you probably compare yourself to others. You question why you are not as lucky as they are. Sometimes you feel inferior or not good enough; sometimes you feel depressed, and sometimes you feel jealous. You see the world as difficult and you feel the world is ignoring you and against you. Other times, you can't understand how people less talented than you become successful. You ask yourself why you are not fulfilling the expectations you have established for yourself. You feel that you don't measure up. The range of outcomes of frustrated expectations has no end.

It is vain to make comparisons. Maybe others have more money or a bigger car than you. Well, maybe they need *that* to fulfill their mission. If you came to paint a house, why would God give you a fancy pen and a desk instead of a fine brush? If you don't trust your talent, you will compare and lament, "Why don't I get the pen and the desk?"

Always, always, whatever we encounter in our lives is perfect and for our own good. If you consider that your life's trajectory has been designed before your birth in favor of your evolution, and if what you inadvertently attract is based on your memories, everything can serve you as an opportunity to let go. There is no place for "bad luck." But for this we must empty our minds of all our obsessive thoughts, ideas, concepts and expectations.

Don't criticize and complain. Don't compare yourself to others. Decide to become aware, drop the heavy baggage you have been carrying all your life, and say *Thank you*. Say *Thank you* for the unbearable companion, the grumpy boss, the incompetent employee, the broken relationship, the dwindling bank account and for being laid off. And of course say *Thank you* to all the "good," "positive" and enjoyable aspects of your life too. Say *Thank you* to everything and everyone at all moments. You cannot imagine how things will change. In fact, you do not have to imagine it—just experience it!

Forgiveness Will Set You Free

Have you noticed how easily children forgive? When two kids have a problem, five minutes later, they are playing together. They let go of their conflict, start again and move on to the important work of the day: playing and enjoying life!

Forgiveness is the possibility of a new start. When you forgive easily, you get back to Zero Frequency® *easily*. And when we are at Zero, everything is possible. Can you see how that works? At Zero, we are children again; we are open, flexible and curious and we don't have resentments, worries or expectations.

If you are awake, if you know who you really are, you will have no problem forgiving yourself and others. It´s easier than you think. You do not need to learn it because we were born knowing how to do it; it´s something natural within us.

In Ho´oponopono, you don't need to tell the other person that you forgive them. This is because what we see outside of us are only our thoughts about the people or situations around us. There is nobody out there doing anything to you. Nothing that is happening now has to do with what is happening in this moment. Everything is about memories and programs, and only you can erase them. People in your life come to give you one more chance to forgive yourself in your heart and set yourself free.

Forgiveness in Ho´oponopono is inner work, and that is much easier than telling someone you forgive them. Rather than focus on verbal or written statements of forgiveness, you work with that which exists within you and with the thoughts you have about the other person and/or that particular situation. In Ho'oponopono, every time those situations appear in our lives, we mentally repeat: "I´m sorry. Please forgive me for whatever is in me that has created this." We accept one hundred percent responsibility—not blame—so we can set ourselves free and come back to Zero Frequency®.

This is simple and tremendously effective inner work because what is erased from us is erased from others and especially from our family, relatives and even our ancestors.

Of course, the most important thing is to forgive ourselves. In Ho´oponopono, we never know which memories we are working with. Through this work, we give permission to a part of us that knows perfectly what we are ready to let go of and erase moment by moment. We all have limiting thoughts that we may not be conscious of, thoughts that become obstacles we put in our own way, such as: "I don't deserve it," or, "I don't have enough education," or, "I was born poor and I'm going to die poor." Although they are at a subconscious level, these thoughts control us and make decisions for us all the time. Many of these thoughts come from the bad habit of comparing ourselves to others and trying to be perfect.

Pain is inevitable, but suffering is optional. It has nothing to do what it was done or said to you. A problem is a problem only if you say it is. In fact, the problem is not the problem. The real problem is how you react to the situation. When you forgive like a child, you let go of the problem and open up possibilities for new connections and new adventures.

You will notice that in almost all ancient philosophies, forgiveness is one of the keys to experiencing the peace and happiness we all long for; it sets us free. Forgiveness also opens the door to prosperity. Think about it. How can you live a truly prosperous life if you are trapped in the memories and emotions of the past? How can you see a path toward true abundance when you are focused on the broken paths you once traveled?

You might have heard the superb saying, "Resentment is like drinking poison and then waiting for the other person to die." That quote has been attributed to many people, yet it originates in Alcoholics Anonymous literature, as written by Emmet Fox. If this philosophy can help people free themselves from the chaos of addiction, it can certainly help you free yourself from your own pain. When you withhold forgiveness from someone, you carry that person and your resentments with you for the rest of your life—or until you *do* forgive them.

I love this passage from *Jesus CEO: Using Ancient Wisdom for Visionary Leadership* by Laurie Beth Jones: "Forgiveness is like the oil in an engine. It keeps the wheels moving. Forgiveness is like gravity... invisible in its power yet profound in its effects."

Why wait? Start forgiving now.

Becoming a Child Again

Two years ago, I was giving a conference in Belgrade, Serbia, and a ten-year-old girl raised her hand and asked, "Mabel, can we talk to animals?"

I looked at her and responded with a question: "Why do you ask? Can you talk to animals?"

She said, "Yes."

"Never change," I told her. "Dare to be different." I then pointed to the hundred people in the audience and said, "They cannot talk to animals and they consider themselves 'normal.' You are right and they are all wrong. Trust yourself. Don't ask others."

Pablo Picasso once said, "Every child is an artist. The problem is how to remain an artist after he grows up." Many artists return to the world of their childhood as Inspiration for their work and ideas. This works for everyone, not just artists. As kids, we see infinite possibilities in unending colors and textures and sounds. The world is full of magic and promise. But growing up, we become so set in our ways that we become closed-minded, unable to conceive new concepts and ideas. Even though the world changes every day, we are not willing to adapt, be more flexible and see things with new eyes. Our sight has become opaque because of the many layers of conditioning. We often become so closed off that we cannot even recognize a good idea when it stares us in the face or when someone else presents it to us.

Dr. Wayne Dyer's daughter, Saje Dyer, was five years old when she contracted flat warts on her face. After a long time suffering and many trips to the doctor, her dermatologist recommended "last option" aggressive treatments. Because the treatments would have lasting negative effects, her parents refused to try them. Instead, they suggested she speak to her illness, and she did!

Saje said, *"I love you* and I appreciate you and what you're here for, but we cannot be together anymore, and you have to go."

In four days, the bumps completely disappeared! She decided not to resist them anymore and just sent them love!

Saje later shared, "As adults, you want something so badly and you don't manifest it into your life. See, as a child I knew this was going to work, that my bumps would go away, because my parents had told me that they would, and I believed them. That was a good source for me. When I spoke to [my bumps] at night, there was no doubt in mind that it was going to work, there was no fear that I would have to go back to the doctor. My parents suggested I talk to my bumps, and for me, this was my third medication option. As adults, you want something so badly, you fear you will not have it; you cannot manifest something that way. You just have to know. This is what I learned for myself as a child. Even now when I want something, and it's not working, I remember the way I was as a child, and knew it would work."

When we are children, we are not engaged in obsessive thinking. Such thinking would mean that we have problems from previous decisions and experiences. It would mean living in the past and in the future, and it would mean that we don't trust ourselves. However, the world of children is full of magic because magic requires living in the present, moment by moment, which is where children live and we can too! We can be an adult and take care of "business" while at the same time maintaining a childlike "happy" attitude toward the world, a renewed vision, moment by moment, every day.

Becoming a child again is the magic that returns you to Zero Frequency®, the place of pure, unfettered awareness you were born in and lived in as a child. That child is still inside you just waiting for you to reconnect. Get the intellect out of the way. Have the courage to stop interfering. It will take you back to your inner core, the place where you wake up and rediscover the ancient, lost wisdom of your heart, the wisdom you have forgotten and replaced with intellectual knowledge. This is not to say that knowledge is not important, but it should not replace the joy and magic of being childlike: uninhibited, joyful and full of promise.

Connect to ZERO *frequency*

You may know the saying, "Sing like no one is listening, dance like nobody's watching, and live like it's heaven on earth." Reconnecting to the freedom and limitlessness you once knew is an effective way to get to Zero Frequency®. Your child is not totally gone and you will be a real grown-up when you recover the child in you. Better still, you will be able to experience more of the magic of life when you get out of your comfort zone and let your child loose, when you become joyful and innocent again.

Here are a few practices that will help you become a child again:

1. Try to remember what you used to dream about. What were your dreams when you were a child and were not fearful? What were your dreams before you neglected your inner child and became like everybody else? What were your dreams when you knew everything was possible? Be willing and open to reconnect with that child in you.

2. Reconnect to what you used to love: Eat things you loved to eat as a child. Go for a walk and skip part of the way. Watch the movies you used to love. Play

on the beach—or in the sand box. Make things. Build things. Color your world.

3. If you are a parent, play more with your children. Sit at the same level, do not impose hierarchies, do not give orders, just PLAY. If you are not a parent, just go to a playground or another place where you can observe and learn from kids playing. Playing with your pets is also a good way to connect with your inner child. Do not worry about what other people think or say about your playing.

4. Laugh as much as you can. And don't forget to breathe!

You can find more resources on how to go back to Zero Frequency® at *www.zerofrequency.com/bookresources*

Chapter 6

Practice Taking Leaps of Faith

Self-trust is the first secret of success.
Ralph Waldo Emerson

After my divorce, I moved into the beautiful townhouse I told you about and that I could not really afford on my own then. When I saw it, I knew God had found it for me. The townhouse had three levels, which allowed space for my kids on one level, communal living space on another level and a place for my work on another level. The grounds surrounding the house were amazing, with beautiful gardens, a swimming pool and lovely walking paths. My teacher used to say, "Whoever designed these grounds was in love." So true! The townhouse was the perfect place for my new life.

A friend had suggested we move in together so we could afford a nicer place. The rent was almost two thousand dollars a month. Before we signed the lease, my friend changed her mind. The "sensible" decision would have been to find something that would fit my budget. Instead, I decided to move forward. I signed the lease by myself, thinking I would find another roommate to help me cover the rent.

I did not find another roommate.

Very soon, my accounting practice started making more money—so much money that I did not *need* a roommate.

I tell you this story not to inspire you to rent or commit to buying something you can't afford, but to show you that, when you trust, God delivers. I didn't wait until I had enough money for the townhouse; I followed my heart, not my mind. I trusted myself and took a leap of faith.

When I got divorced, I told myself, "I don't need to own a house to be happy. I can rent for the rest of my life." I hadn't considered the fact that, when you rent a house, you may have to leave if the owner decides to sell it. That's what happened to me. The owner came to me and said, "Mabel, I know you love this place, but I'm going to put it on the market. I'm giving you notice in case you want to buy it."

Of course I wanted to stay in the beautiful townhouse. I didn't have enough money for the down payment, and I couldn't qualify for a mortgage because I didn't have a long history of stable income. Still, I had been practicing self-trust for several years and so I took another leap of faith. I thought, "If God wants me to stay here, he'll get me the mortgage. If I don't get the mortgage, that means that God has a better place for me." I did not even have to contact a loan agent—the loan agent called me to offer his help! I got the loan, and the house was mine.

These things can happen to anyone—even you—but there is a secret: You need to practice self-trust. Each time you notice you are worrying or thinking too much about something, you must take a leap of faith and give God permission to intervene.

In Chapter 1, I shared the story of my reconnection to self, when I gave myself permission to trust again and follow my heart. I relearned how to take decisions from Inspiration rather than from my intellect (ego). I made "illogical" decisions, and guess what? Those decisions provided me with the best results. The more

I practiced self-trust, the more God provided. I took one leap of faith after another—first my divorce, then starting my own accounting practice, then leaving my successful business to help people through speaking, training and writing. Along the way were many other leaps of faith, too many to count. All of them—yes, all of them—ultimately resulted in more happiness, peace and abundance in my life.

When I chose to let go of my accounting profession and dedicate my life to helping people have more joyful and successful lives, the logical plan would have been to start when I had a reasonable amount of savings. Although those were not my circumstances, I made the decision to do it anyway. Actually, changing from a successful career to a completely different career with no guarantee it would work was even more "illogical," but I knew it was the right choice for me.

What was it that allowed me to be so "courageous" and do these things? Just one thing: trust. I valued my life and I knew that my choices were not only for my own personal benefit, but for the benefit of all. It was not because "it was me," but rather because, when we take a leap of faith and let Divinity guide us, we affect everybody in a good way.

"Trust" Is the Magic Word

Since nothing that happens is a mere coincidence, one day I unexpectedly received a free audio by Napoleon Hill. I decided to listen to it. Napoleon Hill was one of the first self-improvement and personal success writers. Many self-improvement courses are based on his teachings, especially those relying on the mind, such as neuro-linguistic programming (NLP).

In the audio, Napoleon Hill spoke about various spiritual subjects, and of such concepts as abundance and success, which nowadays have become the theme for many spiritual leaders, authors and speakers. After listening to that audio, I started reading Napoleon Hill's works and found something very interesting about trust. He considers it essential for success. He says that trust is one of those things that cannot be taught but can be built by autosuggestion, that we first must begin to trust, and that, the more we practice trust, the more we "hypnotize" ourselves into it, the more it will become second nature to us.

Trusting became my practice. Whenever I heard those tiny voices telling me that I wasn't good enough or that I couldn't do it, or whenever I was in a difficult or scary situation, I would choose to stop all the stories in my mind by telling myself, "I am going to let go and trust!" I had actually been doing autosuggestion without knowing it!

Napoleon Hill provides a slightly macabre but very interesting example of how autosuggestion works. He says that those who kill for the first time feel as though they can hardly bear to be in their body. They feel tremendous anguish. When they kill a second time, they feel uncomfortable but not as much as the first time. And once they've killed several times, they feel nothing. Killing doesn't affect them anymore. Hill uses this as an example of autosuggestion. So, why not use the power of autosuggestion to attract a life of peace and happiness? I suggest you try it, because, when you start trusting, you will find the happiness and peace you are looking for. And happy and peaceful people will undoubtedly be successful.

Trusting is a decision and a practice! Our decisions cause consequences in our lives. We change our destinies at any given moment in accordance with our choices. We can choose to react or not react, let go or not let go. This is the question and the secret!

In my life, once I started trusting myself, I found God. For me, God is the part inside me that knows better. It's my connection to the dance and the wisdom of the whole Universe. And it's inside you too! When people don't believe, I ask them, "Who thought of the human body or the flowers and the oceans?" It doesn't matter what you call it, you need to realize there is a more intelligent mind than yours. You have to realize you don't know and become humble.

Have you ever noticed how much we trust the negative? We know that life can change for the worse in a second. We accept the possibility that we may have an accident, be told we have cancer, or suddenly die. Why can't we similarly trust the positive? Why don't we trust that our lives can change for the better in a second? If we become present and conscious and trust our own wisdom, our lives will definitely change for the better, moment by moment.

Why Are You Waiting?

Do you remember the story about the Romanian sisters, Katja and Sylvie? Katja had come to a Ho'oponopono training hoping that I would "fix" her sister Sylvie's mental disability. You might also remember that, at the end of the Zero Frequency® training on the second day, Katja and Sylvie danced along with all of the other attendees. And, I haven't yet shared with you another conversation I had with Katja at the end of that second day.

«"You know, Mabel," she said, "I always wanted to be a dancer, but my father wouldn't let me." Katja went on to explain that she felt she should pursue a more "serious" profession. So she became a physician.

"I'm going to go for it," Katja told me. "I'm going to start dancing."

"Wonderful," I said. "Take your sister. This will be so important for the two of you to enjoy together."

Now, I'm used to hearing similar announcements. Many people come to my Zero Frequency® trainings and classes and come away with a new commitment to joy, which often involves recommitting to a deeply held desire. What *did* surprise me was Katja's response, "What I meant, Mabel, is I'm going to dance professionally. On the stage."

Katja appeared to be in her fifties and now she was going to try to become a professional dancer, long after many dancers have retired. You know, why not? My surprise at her answer revealed my own preconceived notions about career dancers. Who is to say Katja could not realize her dream? That day, she fell back in love with something that had once brought her great joy, and there is great power in a happy pursuit. In her eyes I could see that she had no doubt she would dance on the stage one day.

We often make decisions based on doubt and lack of self-trust. We don't love and accept ourselves. Again and again we look for acceptance from the outside. Of course, if our inner state is lacking in acceptance and trust, what can we expect from the outside?

When you trust yourself, you will also trust life, because, after all, you are here as an expression of Life itself, and Life doesn't believe in waste. It hasn't made the effort to bring you here for no reason. God (the Universe) knows your talents and is waiting for you to decide to manifest them. These talents are never insignificant, although life's circumstances may make you perceive them that way. However, if you follow your heart's desire and you ground yourself in trust, you will be rewarded.

Stephen King's story might inspire you. This successful author has sold more than three hundred million copies of his books. In his book, *On Writing,* he explains his trajectory as a writer. There he tells us how, when he was still a teenager, he kept publishers' rejection notices pinned on his wall. When the pin became insufficient to hold the weight of the rejection notes, King substituted a hook and continued writing. It's clear that, just like many other successful entrepreneurs, Stephen King possessed an unshakeable trust in himself. I hope you also develop the required trust.

Remember this: You are here for a reason and you are unique! Never stop acknowledging the light you have within you and never underestimate your talents. I hope you decide to overcome your fears and doubts so you can have the strength to start trusting, and the strength and energy to follow your calling. The world is waiting for you.

In 2015, Karmen, my organizer in Croatia, wrote me, "Mabel, the publisher here says there is not enough time to publish your latest book by the time you'll be coming to present in Zagreb; what do you think if I publish it myself?"

I told her, "Go ahead."

Karmen had organized a free introductory conference in Zagreb. I was scheduled to speak about the book and sign copies. When I arrived, she handed me a copy of my book. That was the first time I saw the actual book printed in the Croatian language. It looked professionally done and beautiful. She had done a great job.

As I was talking to people at the conference, I said, "Look at the great job she did! You know what the most interesting part of this is? She is not a professional publisher and I am not a professional writer!" Isn't it ironic? The "professional" publisher had said it could not be done on time. And there I was in front of these people, without any background or study in writing books nor in public speaking, holding my book in my hands.

So the question I asked them and I want to ask you, is: What are you waiting for? What do you think you are lacking which is an impediment to doing what you really love and want to do?

You need to stop thinking and jump, because God knows exactly "how" you are going to do it. He is just waiting for you to take the first step. You need to get out of your comfort zone, feel the fear and then do it anyway. Believe me, when you trust and you want it so badly that you're willing to do whatever it takes, everything falls into place and everything happens effortlessly. You will look back and you will not believe your life. You will feel that you hardly had to do much.

What is your ego (the crazy of the house) telling you? Do you believe you don't have enough education? Enough money? Are you still "thinking" about it?

Listening and believing to what other people say you should be doing? There is nothing to think, to know or to worry about. You already have everything you need to fulfill your mission because when you are using your innate talents, you will know why you are doing it, you will be happy and you will be doing something good for everybody, because you matter. And please, do not concern yourself with "how." Divinity knows *how*, and is just waiting for you.

Connect to **ZERO** *frequency*

The message is that we must wake up and realize who we really are. But how do we start? I get asked this question a lot. The first step is as easy as this: Decide you are going to trust and begin practicing. I understand this is the opposite of what you have been doing. I know I am asking you to trust in the unknown, and this will be very uncomfortable and scary in the beginning. But believe me, it will become like second nature, and you will love the results if you really let go and trust. You will also be giving a clear message to your inner child about what you are choosing and practicing now. Clarity is a *must*.

Here are a few suggestions to help you begin practicing leaps of faith:

1. Mentally repeat to yourself: "I let go and trust; I let go and trust." What you are doing is autosuggestion. This means that you are consciously choosing to let go and trust moment by moment. If you are aware, you will make different decisions, you will be less reactive and your decisions and actions will come from the *part in you that knows* best— Inspiration, instead of programming. This is the way to let go and let God, to start building the trusting muscle.

2. Allow yourself to receive Inspiration throughout your whole being. Allow it to fill your every cell and pour through every pore. If you feel the stimulus, the Inspiration, *trust* it! Don't pay attention to your ego, let go and you will soon be ready to embark on the adventure. The conditions will become right; there is nothing you need to know. This special part in you has the "know-how." Just remain vigilant so you're sure not to miss the opportunities that come your way. Be open, alert and flexible.

3. As Joseph Campbell put it: "My general formula for my students is 'Follow your bliss.' Find where

it is, and don't be afraid to follow it." Stay at Zero Frequency®, a state of flowing, as much as you can. This state happens when you are happy for no specific reason. Similar to the state achieved in meditation, it is where you can observe and enjoy. What this state feels like varies from person to person. To get to it, simply say, "STOP" when you realize you are looking for happiness in the outside world. Enjoy the outside. Play going in and out of this state, have fun and do not allow your emotional state to affect you. "STOP" and be present and allow Divinity to arrange perfect happenings for you.

4. Do the "rocking chair" exercise. Imagine you are ninety years old, sitting in a rocking chair and reflecting on your life. You are relaxed and content, satisfied with all of your choices. You have accomplished and experienced everything you dreamed of, and now recalling the special moments brings you joy. Think back to the moments that made you smile. Remember how you used your unique talents and how trusting made a difference in your life. Imagine your ninety-year-old self can talk to you *now*. What would you say? How would you advise yourself? Now tell yourself about the

impact you've made on the world. What is the legacy you want to leave to others?

5. Take a deep breath and relax. See yourself enjoying the sunset overlooking the ocean. A young person is coming toward you. As it gets closer, you realize it is you, the adolescent version of you. What advice do you give to your younger self? What would help your younger self to be happier? To trust more? To experience more of life? To be free?

You can find more resources on how to go back to Zero Frequency® at *www.zerofrequency.com/bookresources*

Chapter 7

Practice Gratitude

Gratitude is not only the greatest of virtues,
but the parent of all others.
Cicerón

D o you know the story of God and the shoemaker? Sometimes, the story is told as Jesus and the shoemaker; sometimes, the minor details change, but the meaning is the same. The story goes like this…

God, taking the form of a homeless man, went to see the shoemaker and asked him to repair the shoes he was wearing. He said, "I am so poor that I only have one pair of shoes, and, as you can see, they are ripped and useless. I don't have money to pay you for the repair, but would you fix them for me?"

The shoemaker said, "I don't work for free. I am also poor, and that repair will cost me money."

"I am God," the homeless man replied. "If you fix my shoes, I can give you whatever you want."

The shoemaker did not trust the man. He said, "Can you give me the million dollars I need to be happy?"

God said, "I can give you one million dollars, but, in return, you must give me your legs."

"And what good is one million dollars if I have no legs?"

God replied, "I can give you five million dollars if you give me your arms."

"And what can I do with five million if I won't even be able to eat on my own?"

God said, "I can give you fifty million dollars if you give me your eyes."

The shoemaker, who had grown increasingly agitated, said, "And tell me, what could I do with so much money if I could not see the world or see the faces of my wife and children?"

God smiled at the shoemaker and said, "Oh, my son, how can you say you are poor? I offered you fifty-six million dollars, and you did not accept it in exchange for the healthy parts of your body.

Do you not see that you are rich and haven't even noticed it?".

Like the shoemaker, we often don't realize how much we already have. We narrowly define wealth, not realizing how wealthy we truly are. Wealthy in love, in health, in friendship, in passion, in nature, in beauty and in time. The shoemaker didn't realize how much he already had to say *thank you* for. And, he didn't realize how his life, despite his financial poverty, could have been much, much worse. We rarely appreciate what we have until it is taken away from us or until there is a possibility that we will have to give it up.

Practicing gratitude calls on us to recognize all we have, and appreciate it. Be thankful for it. When you practice gratitude, no matter your circumstances, you open yourself to the field of all possibilities that is Zero Frequency®.

Often, we do not feel gratitude for what we have because we are always concentrating on what we think we are lacking. Our mind tells us that we know how and when things should happen. Therefore, when reality does not meet our expectations, we become angry and close our hearts. In so doing, we are unable to see the wonders of life.

You see, we are very good at complaining and blaming. We focus on everything that did not go well and the times we failed. It justifies our being unhappy and stuck. However, if we stop for a moment and look at the sky, a tree, the smile of a child, or smell the scent of a rose, we'll begin to appreciate the beauty around us. We'll realize how fortunate we are, and good things will begin to come into our lives. We take our lives for granted and tend to forget the immense power of gratitude. We don't stop to appreciate that we can breathe without artificial help or stand on our two feet or that we have our two arms and don't depend on others to bathe or get dressed. Being part of this world is a great privilege and opportunity, and we must find the way to feel appreciation and gratitude for the mere fact of being alive, no matter what.

Being grateful requires less energy and time than complaining. Almost immediately, we feel lighter, happier and very different from the feelings triggered when we complain. Gratitude will raise your vibration and is the fastest way to connect to Zero Frequency®.

Good Luck or Bad Luck?

Have you heard the story about the storms and the crop? It is a wonderful story that perfectly exemplifies what it means to live in the present without judgments.

One day, a farmer asked God, "Please let me rule over nature so that my crops can be more profitable." God agreed. When the farmer wanted rain, it came. When he asked for the bright beautiful sun, it shone as directed. Whatever weather he asked for, he received. Except at harvest, when he was surprised to discover that his efforts did not yield the riches he expected.

The farmer asked God why his plan failed. God replied, "You asked for what you wanted, but not for what was needed. You never asked for storms, which are necessary to clean the crops, to keep away the birds and animals that destroy them and to purify them from plagues that destroy them."

The moral here is that we never know if an event is a blessing or a misfortune. So better not get attached to one or the other nor rejoice for one and lament the other. Reality is always in the eye of the beholder. Remember, the intellect doesn't have the whole picture; just say *Thank you* to whatever comes your way and let it go. Please know that the Universe's plans are always perfect, and there is no such thing as good or bad luck.

A Different Understanding of Our Challenges

Be grateful for your adversities; they are always a blessing in disguise. There is no coincidence, for example, as to who would be your boss, your peer or your subordinate. Those people and situations are not there by chance, and, the more challenging they are, the bigger the opportunity and the greater the reward, if we choose to let go instead of react!

If we talk about the Divine plan for our professional life and career, everything could be an opportunity in your life to start something different and better based on the authentic yearnings of your soul and your most brilliant talents, and sometimes the only way forward is to have you lose it all, or to fire you, because you would be too comfortable and not move on your own.

While I was teaching a seminar in Barcelona, a student shared a personal story. He said, "You know Mabel, at one point I was a millionaire and then I lost everything. I actually owe a lot of money now. When I was a multimillionaire, the only thing I did was to work, work, work. I considered myself a very important person, doing very important things. So for example, I didn't spend time with my little daughter because I was busy doing 'important' things. Do you know what, Mabel? Now I spend more time with my daughter, and this time is precious to me! I am grateful. I connect with nature. I appreciate things I never appreciated before."

Do you want to move forward? Do you want to attract great things in your life? Start by being grateful. Be grateful for the good things and the bad things. Say yes to your adversities. Adversities make you stronger and better and open new doors for you.

An episode of *The Oprah Winfrey Show* stayed with me, and I still remember it to this day. She had a husband and wife as guests, and the husband had been laid off. But when he came home and told his wife, she said, "Let's open a champagne bottle and celebrate." Then she suggested they don't tell anyone about it. A week later, he was offered a new job that paid better and that he loved and enjoyed much more. And this was in the middle of the big recession!

See, if you let go instead of complaining, worrying and talking about it, God performs miracles. But please do not wait until you lose everything or you touch bottom to realize what is important in life. You have already begun to practice responsibility, so this will come easier for you. And you have probably also begun to see how some seemingly unfortunate circumstances have turned out to be blessings, so gratitude for everything in your life will also be easier for you. Do you see how the Zero Frequency® practices become easier and easier?

Be grateful for what you have now!

The Time Is Now

On November 4, 1962, President John F. Kennedy issued the customary Thanksgiving proclamation in honor of the US national holiday to come later that month. Here is an excerpt:

> "Today we give our thanks, most of all, for the ideals of honor and faith we inherit from our forefathers—for the decency of purpose, steadfastness of resolve and strength of will, for the courage and the humility, which they possessed and which we must seek every day to emulate. As we express our gratitude, we must never forget that the highest appreciation is not to utter words but to live by them.
>
> Let us therefore proclaim our gratitude to Providence for manifold blessings—let us be humbly thankful for inherited ideals—and let us resolve to share those blessings and those ideals with our fellow human beings throughout the world.

On that day let us gather in sanctuaries dedicated to worship and in homes blessed by family affection to express our gratitude for the glorious gifts of God; and let us earnestly and humbly pray that He will continue to guide and sustain us in the great unfinished tasks of achieving peace, justice, and understanding among all men and nations and of ending misery and suffering wherever they exist."

I wanted to share this excerpt with you because now it is time to walk our talk. We must start living in gratitude, appreciate what we have and stop comparing what we have to what other people have. We have to start living at Zero Frequency®, so that we can, as President Kennedy said, "end misery and suffering wherever they exist"—beginning with our own lives.

Connect to ZERO *frequency*

Did you know you that you can develop your feelings of gratitude through practice? In a study at Indiana State University, researchers studied the effects of gratitude exercise on forty-three people who suffered from anxiety and depression. Half of the group was instructed to write thank-you letters. Then the entire group underwent brain scans. Those who completed the gratitude exercise showed more "gratitude-related activity" in their brains, which basically means they experienced the feeling of gratitude more readily and more often.

Gratitude practice does not have to take much time. It only takes a minute to stop and make note of three things for which you are deeply grateful. Here are some suggestions for your own gratitude practice:

1. Make a list of all the things that you are grateful for in your life or at least in the last twelve months. You can feel thankful both for adversity and for joy. Very often, great blessings only come to us through adverse experiences. I encourage you to look for the gifts in your life, whether they come from adversity or from joy, and embrace gratitude before you leave this stage of your life behind.

2. Then begin a daily practice of listing all the things you can be grateful for that day. If you have the time, do this in the morning and at night. Always take it with you and keep adding to it every time you notice or realize something or someone to be grateful for. You might also consider setting a reminder on your phone or computer that calls

on you to take a moment to notice what you are grateful for in that moment. When you are focused on the simple gifts of life, you will soon discover you are surrounded by wonders and blessings!

3. When you are caught up in a situation, or trying to solve a problem, remind yourself that there is a blessing behind it. Mentally make a list: "The things I can be grateful for because this is happening..." New insights and knowledge can be gained from any challenge. More importantly, you will be changing your frequency, going to Zero.

You can find more resources on how to go back to Zero Frequency® at *www.zerofrequency.com/bookresources*

Chapter 8

Practice Letting Go

Giving up is "There, it's over."
Letting go, "I've just begun!"
Suzanne Marshall Lucas

A few years ago, I decided to take tango dance lessons, because I wanted to learn how to allow myself to be led by a man. In the dance of the tango, the man always leads, and the woman has to let the man guide her. This did not come naturally for me, and I needed some practice.

As the weeks of the class flew by, I began to notice a pattern. Every time I really let go and allowed my partner to lead, I looked like a pro, and it felt like magic. The problem was, sometimes I couldn't go with the flow and got stuck in my head. When I paid attention to the dance, when I was thinking and not observing, I stumbled. Trying to remember the routine, I would focus on the next step and the one after that. Or I would wonder, "Am I doing it right?" And each time, I would lose my footing.

For me, this was a great lesson—more than I was expecting from my tango class! So often we cause a lot of problems for ourselves because we are stuck in our heads. By now you know, the head—the intellect—creates problems. We think, we plan, we worry, we wonder about outcomes and—just like that—we stumble. We resist, instead of letting go. When we fret about how well we're doing, we call it "trying hard" or "caring deeply" and we believe that we will accomplish more or do better because of this. In actuality, this way of thinking holds us back. In the ancient Indian scriptures, the Vedas, the principle of "the economy of effort" explains how ideas become reality easily, *without trying*. In his book, *The Seven Spiritual Laws of Success,* Deepak Chopra calls it "The Law of Least Effort." When we let go, this law kicks in, and suddenly we move gracefully through the world, like a dancer. We manifest what we deeply desire effortlessly.

You may feel as though you have been "stumbling" through your life for quite some time, always wondering if you're "doing it right." When you lose your footing in life, just as in the tango, it's because you are out of the flow. The only solution is to let go of control and allow the Universe to lead.

I experienced the flow when I let go and I allowed my partner to guide me across the dance floor. You've felt it before; we all have. Chopra explains that nature works effortlessly. So the flow is not illusive or rare. You can feel it simply by practicing letting go.

Sometimes, it's difficult to let go, because we are presented with outcomes we did not expect. Other times, fear takes hold and feels stronger than Zero, even though it's not. This is why it is so important for you trust being in the flow!

Let Go of What?

We must let go of the "I know" syndrome and all the opinions, judgments, expectations, interpretations and beliefs from our past! This leads us to the real question. How well do you allow your subconscious mind (the computer bank) to influence your conscious mind (the part in you that is easily defined as you)? This, it turns out, is the key to personal greatness.

In his book, *The User Illusion,* Tor Norretranders details interviews with retired football star Joe Montana and Danish soccer star Michael Laudrup, the World Cup hero. They both say that they were never consciously aware when making their biggest plays. Or, if they were thinking, it was only to plot their moves while their subconscious took care of the real business. This principle applies to artists, executives, lawyers and teachers—to virtually everyone. All of us have had great moments when we've acted without thinking (let go) and produced something truly impressive. My best writing has come when I just sat down and wrote without consciously guiding my thoughts. Most songwriters prepare to get themselves into a similar state so their songs would simply come to them. Those highly gifted people figured out the way to allow their subconscious to cooperate with their conscious minds. Or, to use sporting terminology, these folks know how to get into "The Zone."

Zero Frequency® is the state of being in The Zone—a zone in which everything flows and everything is possible.

Have you ever had the experience that "time flies"? If you pay attention, you'll notice that this always happens when you're doing something you love, when you are at Zero. At those times, your subconscious is at full force, while your conscious mind is taking a break. You become totally immersed in the activity you are performing; you are "there," completely present. When you let go, you experience time differently. This place of no static and no resistance is so powerful it alters our perception of time.

Set Yourself Free from Expectations

During a full-day Zero Frequency® training in Basel, Switzerland, a student came in after the first break and said, "I thought we were going to experience Zero Frequency® in this seminar."

Talk about preconceived ideas and expectations! I looked at him and said, "First, give me a chance. We just went through barely two hours of training. We have most of the work ahead of us. And most importantly, how do you know that you are not at Zero? Maybe you were, and you didn't know it. One thing is clear: As soon as you have a question, an expectation and/or a judgment, you are definitely not at Zero."

I went on to tell him, "What would be the point of taking you back to Zero here today? Tomorrow, when you go back to work or when you have to interact with difficult people in your life, you will not be able to recreate that state. I'd rather show you how you can do it on your own, so you won't need me or anyone outside yourself to enter The Zone."

Most important is to be aware when you *are not* at Zero Frequency®, so you can choose to let go and tune yourself to the right frequency.

To have an expectation means to be attached to a particular way in which we figure events should happen. Expectations lead you to think you know more about how things should be than the Universe. This can only slow you down and lead you to unnecessary frustrations. It blocks your connection with Inspiration. You are not in balance, you feel stuck and, yes, you are definitely stuck in the past or the future. *Therefore, you stumble.*

Expectations lead you to focus outside yourself and take you out of the present. You are continually checking whether what is happening is what "should" be happening. The solution is to realize that everything is perfect, that we are perfect just the way we are. As I've said before and will say many times to come, we must always remember that we are one hundred percent responsible for the reality we are manifesting and that we have the control and the means to change it. God always gives us everything we need to fulfill our purpose.

I shared this with you in Chapter 4, and it bears repeating: Please do not confuse responsibility with guilt. We are one hundred percent responsible for our reality because everything is just memories replaying in our subconscious mind. The good news is that since they are inside you, you can choose to let go and set yourself free from them. You created it; you can change it. It is not that you're bad and guilty; you are just responsible and you can do something about it! When you stop blaming and start letting go, you are actually taking control.

Anything that appears to be an impediment presents an opportunity to see what we are ready to let go of. God is not going to force you to face something that is not in resonance with your current state of consciousness, something that you are not yet ready to let go of. This would be useless and even counterproductive. What the Order of God does is to ensure that the perfect thing will happen so we can continue releasing memories and grow.

When the time comes in which we are sufficiently free of the clutches of the ego, miracles will begin to manifest more and more. Well, miracles happen all the time. But if you are focusing on what doesn't work, or what you think you are lacking, you will miss the miracles, because they will not be tangible. You see, miracles do not occur "outside;" they take place within you. The peace, happiness and freedom you experience despite all the problems you may have is the utmost miracle. I assure you that these are the miracles that really count. To be able to detach and not react to painful memories—to be able to delete them—is the best investment we can make for ourselves, for our families, relatives and ancestors. It is like paying back a debt in order to set ourselves free.

I have a personal story about expectations. After taking the Ho'oponopono training four or five times in the first six months after I had discovered it, I went to Dr. Hew Len and I said, "I let go and keep letting go, but it doesn't work."

First, he didn't say anything, but later he came to me, looked into my eyes and said, "No expectations." See, he waited for Inspiration to tell him what I could hear and understand at the right moment. Not only did I understand, it brought me so much peace! Sure, my intellect didn't know what was right. I just had to let go of the expectations and keep going. Please know, I still have expectations, but I know it's my intellect making stories. I say to myself, "*Thank you* but no thank you. I am not buying expectations anymore."

Being aware of the Universe's perfection will keep us in a constant attitude of awe and wonder. But for this we must let go of our expectations and dedicate ourselves to free ourselves from thinking so much. We must always remember that God knows more than we do and wants what is best for us. In fact, He has more in store for us than we can ever imagine or visualize. That's why God makes us move along paths that sometimes seem strange to us. If we become humble and release expectations, comparisons, complaining and the need to be right all the time and if we trust, we will connect with Zero Frequency®. In this perfect state, we will be in the flow, we will move forward and we will realize that God's time is the perfect time.

Letting Go Is Not Giving Up

Yes, you can "let go and let God" (or the Universe or whatever name you choose), even when you don't understand exactly why something is happening. Our perception of everything and everyone is limited because we see through the filters of our memories. You need to clean your "glasses" and learn to see without the fog. Only then, will you be able to see the bigger picture.

Please do not confuse letting go with giving up. Giving up is putting an end to dreams, desires, projects—sometimes to life itself. Letting go opens the door to Inspiration and endless possibilities. Letting go is going back to Zero, to a new beginning, to a new start. When you let go, you tune into Zero Frequency®, the state of total awareness of the present moment, and you can hear the voice of the Universe that brings you peace, happiness and perfect solutions.

Consider Deepak Chopra's sixth spiritual law of success, "The Law of Detachment." He explains that, when we let go of our attachment to something we want, we receive what we want. He makes it clear that The Law of Detachment does not mean letting go of your intention or your desire; it simply means you are letting go of the outcome. When you are attached to a specific outcome, it is a sign that you are afraid of uncertainty, that you don't truly trust the power of your authentic self.

According to Chopra, attachment comes from "poverty consciousness" and detachment comes from "wealth consciousness." This is an important distinction. I've experienced this myself, and you have too. Think about the last time you created something wonderful in your life, without effort.

Instead of fixating on specific, measurable outcomes, you remained open, and perhaps the outcome was even better than you could have imagined, even more marvelous than you ever hoped it could be. Then, as if by magic, everything slotted into place. You might have even called it a miracle, or grace or divine intervention. Do you remember that experience? Remember how you felt about it: as if you were connected to the Universe, as if you were working alongside God? That experience and those feelings were possible because you let go of attachment and trusted.

Similarly, you can let go of your attachment to your environment, to pain and to negative outcomes. People endure and survive the most heinous acts and horrible tragedies in part because of how they choose to view their reality. In his book, *The Seven Habits of Highly Effective People,* Steven Covey shares the story of Victor Frankl, a Jew imprisoned in the Nazi death camps in Germany who lost every family member except his sister and endured unspeakable torture. You may have heard Frankl talk about the moment he realized he still had one freedom that the Nazis could not take from him—his ability to decide how an experience would affect him. He called this "the last of human freedoms."

I mention Covey because I want to share a passage from his book in which he talks about Frankl. "In the midst of the most degrading circumstances imaginable, Frankl used the human endowment of self-awareness to discover a fundamental principle about the nature of man: Between stimulus and response, man has the freedom to choose. Within the freedom to choose are those endowments that make us uniquely human. In addition to self-awareness, we have imagination— the ability to create in our minds beyond our present reality. We have conscience—a deep inner awareness of right and wrong, of the principles that govern our behavior, and a sense of the degree to which our thoughts and actions are in harmony with them. And we have independent will—the ability to act based on our self-awareness, free of all other influences."

You, too, have this will. You can choose how you react to a situation. You can let go of the suffering. You can even let go of the reality of your current circumstances. How you choose to react to the world is up to you, and no one can take that away *or do it for you.* It is your right. You have free choice.

You might not be able to change the circumstances, but circumstances are always neutral, and you have the power to change the way you think, feel and act about them. Change your thoughts about something and you change your results (consequences). Change your thoughts; you might end up with a happier and more fulfilling ending.

Would You Rather Win or Be Happy?

Many people write to me to share the impact of practicing living at Zero Frequency®. One of my favorite testimonials came from Guillermina, who had been in the process of getting divorced. Her soon-to-be ex-husband had refused to meet with her or speak with her, and so the process was repeatedly delayed.

Guillermina wrote, "I had my divorce hearing today. The judge explained that, since the parties did not agree, she would reschedule the hearing for September. Without thinking, I spoke up. I said, 'Your honor, do you think I can wait until September simply because this man does not want to communicate with me? Please listen to what I have to say. I don't have until September to be happy! I claim my happiness today! I just want to let go and trust today!' The judge looked at me, surprised. I wasn't sure if she understood anything I said."

Understand that Guillermina had not planned to say what she said or anything at all; if she had thought about it beforehand or second-guessed herself when she got the impulse, she may not have raised her concerns at all.

A few moments passed, and then the judge instructed the other attorney to bring her ex forward, because, even if he didn't want to speak with her, he would have to at least *listen* to her when *she* spoke.

Guillermina wrote, "He came in like a rat, with his head down. I started talking. I believe what I said was perfect and correct. However, my ex did not accept any of my petitions. Still, my only response was, 'Thank you! Thank you! Thank you!' My attorney wanted to defend me, to get my ex to change his mind, but I told her, 'Can you be quiet? Everything is perfect and correct. I am letting go.' I knew that God was there, guiding everything."

In the end, Guillermina was granted her divorce, but her ex got everything he wanted. Technically, she lost her case, because she did not get the results she had been fighting for. Still, she agreed to everything and did not resist. In her testimony she wrote, "I had the joy of telling my ex, 'you won.' I reflected on life, and thought, 'What do we take when we die? Nothing at all!' Even though in his eyes and in the eyes of the law, he won, it's not about winning or losing. It's about having peace. And today, God gave that to me on a platter!"

When the hearing was over, Guillermina greeted her ex's attorney with a hug and said, "Thank you! Thank you! Thank you!" Her own attorney was still not over the shock of the judge changing her mind about moving the hearing to September. And when Guillermina saw her ex one last time, she said, "Don't get close to me. I'm done. This is the end."

Then her lawyer said to her, "It's too bad you couldn't greet him at the end."

"Too bad for you!" Guillermina said. "It's the first time in twenty-four years and four months that I said to him, 'I'm done!' THANK YOU!"

At the end, Guillermina wrote to me: "Today I spent the day crying, but with the certainty that God squeezes but does not strangle!"

Some people would call the outcome of Guillermina's divorce a failure, but it's not, nor does she view it that way. Zero Frequency® does not guarantee we will get the results we want. When we practice abundance (and letting go), we are not concerned with the outcome. We trust, we take action and we are happy no matter what happens.

Another lesson from Guillermina's story is our need to be right, which we also perceive as "winning"— winning an argument, or, in her case, a court battle. Our need to be right or have the last word is one of the most ingrained human characteristics, and it is necessary to radically remove it if we want happiness and peace. Notice that when you think you are right you stubbornly believe your thoughts and your stories without question or doubt. You don't consider that they might be a replay of your old memories and will cause you the same unhappiness as they did in the past. You just want to be dead right! We have a case of confused identity here. We think we must defend our thoughts because we are convinced that we *are* our thoughts. It does not occur to us that we are separate from them, and so we do everything we can to defend our way of thinking.

The fallacy is to think that our thoughts are the truth, when in reality thoughts are but memories and a very limited vision of the truth. Consequently, our limited way of interpreting this "truth" causes us to automatically disregard other people's ideas and visions. We become arrogant, thinking we know best, and engage in a multitude of confrontations and disagreements with others. And this in turn keeps us stuck, attracting exactly the opposite of what we want to attract. In short, our attachment to being right is a big obstacle to our happiness. It prevents us from moving toward peace, and we miss opportunities to open new doors.

It is really up to you whether you choose to continue giving credit to what you think of yourself (your programs) and what you think of others and what is right and wrong or choose to let go of that and recognize that everything is perfect the way it is. You must know that if you choose the former, you will be attracting the same kind of life experiences you've always attracted. I'm reminded of the popular saying: Insanity is doing the same thing over and over and expecting a different result. Again, the answer lies in changing channels. Stop listening to the frequency of righteousness, become more humble, realize that you don't know as much as you think you know and allow yourself to flow with the clarity of God, which is Inspiration and is closer than your own breath. And yes, allowing God to guide us requires humility. It requires the humility to stop thinking or at least stop giving power and control to our thoughts. It is essential to open our minds, be flexible and let go of expectations.

Now remember, when I say God, I mean that *part inside you that really knows better!* You connect with this part every time you choose to listen to your right brain (wisdom) rather than to your left-brain (intellect). Such knowing, without knowing how you know it, is Inspiration. I am not asking you to go one inch outside yourself to find it.

As we become more humble, we recognize that there is a mind much larger and more intelligent than ours, the same mind that created the Universe. It thought up the human body, the oceans, the mountains and the flowers. Humility implies letting go of the attachment to our own thinking and of being convinced that we are right, and instead giving the command to this Great Mind—God and Inspiration—that has the perfect solutions for all our problems.

In this book I've shared quotes from Michael Singer's book, *The Untethered Soul.* I highly recommend you read it as you continue to practice letting go. This quote from his book is appropriate for Guillermina's story: "The energy shifts and variations that take place in the heart, run your life. You are so identified with them that you use words 'I' and 'me' when you are referring to what's going on in your heart. But in truth, you are not your heart. You are the experiencer of your heart. Allow the experiences of life to come in and pass through your being. Let them go. It's that easy. Be happy. Just open, relax your heart, forgive, laugh, or do anything you want. Just don't push them back down."

Letting go works. It sets you free. It gives you peace beyond understanding. You don't need to be right. You do not have to win. You do not have to have the last word. Your happiness, peace and freedom are priceless.

Feel the Fear and Do It Anyway

Deep down, we are afraid because we don't know who we are. We perceive ourselves with our limited thoughts and limited sight. We are afraid because we believe we are alone. We fear the unknown, being rejected, failing, living and dying. We fear too much and trust too little. As a result, we never bet on our passions and don't risk developing our talents. In other words, we don't choose to live and be happy. When you gain insight into your inner essence, you fear nothing. Only then you will be capable of taking risks and trusting the unknown.

Master Jiddu Krishnamurti affirmed that thought, knowledge and time form an inseparable reality, which is the root of all fear. He explained it during a chat he offered in Brockwood Park School near London in 1983: "Time is thought, because thought is the response of memory, which is knowledge and experience. So, knowledge belongs in the realm of time... Therefore, time, thought and knowledge are not separate; they are truly a single movement and this is the cause of fear."

These words of Krishnamurti are an excellent synthesis of what we have been saying about memories as being the source of thoughts and emotions. Now we can also see that memories are specifically identified as the source of fear. Osho, too, said, "If the mind is afraid, it becomes a whirlwind of thoughts." The subject is clear.

How many of us are held back because we are paying attention to someone else's limiting beliefs and fears? Do you know the story about the crabs?

> *A man was walking along the beach and saw another man fishing in the surf with a bait bucket beside him. As he drew closer, he saw that the bait bucket had no lid and had live crabs inside.*
>
> *"Why don't you cover your bait bucket so the crabs won't escape?" he asked.*

"You don't understand," the man replied, "if there was one crab in the bucket it would surely crawl out very quickly. However, when there are many crabs in the bucket, if one tries to crawl up the side, the others grab hold of it and pull it back down so it will share the same fate as the rest of them."

So it is with people. If one tries to do something different, get better grades, improve herself, escape her environment or dream big dreams, there will always be those who will try to drag her back down to share their fate.

Ignore the crabs. Charge ahead and do what is right for you. It may not be easy, and you may not succeed as much as you'd like, but you will *never* share the same fate as those who never try. Feel the fear and do it anyway. The only thing to be afraid of is fear itself! Fears are inevitable. They hide in the background and jump out every time we have to, or want to do something new or different. We must feel the fear and do what we intend to do, no matter what.

Don't Let Regret Hold You Back

In my Zero Frequency® trainings, I ask students to come to the front of the room and write their biggest regret on a chalkboard or whiteboard. As the board fills up, a pattern emerges: Most of the regrets have to do with chances not taken. We tend to regret the things we have not done more than the things we *have* done. It's our unlived life that haunts us, that we carry with us day in and day out like an extra person attached to our backs. The weight is heavy and it keeps us from seeing new paths and different opportunities.

Students look at the regret-filled board and assume that now their task is to go after the idea or dream they set aside. Instead, I give them erasers. As in the exercise I shared in Chapter 3, they erase their regrets, all of them, until the chalkboard is clean. What is left is a fresh space for new plans, *new* ideas and *new* dreams.

Practicing taking a leap of faith does not have to mean picking up projects left unfinished or sending letters you never finished or pursuing interests you long ago left behind. Yes, you wanted to take action at one time and then didn't, but that doesn't mean you have to follow through on those actions to be whole. You can take a leap of faith toward something else, something fresh, something unexpected. Yes, look to your regrets for clues about what you might want to experience or accomplish, but don't let them hold you back from creating a new life.

Claim your regrets, accept them and then move on. You can't go back and change the decisions you've already made; the inaction was a choice. And maybe, just maybe, it was actually the right choice. Maybe it was the *perfect* choice. Eckart Tolle said, "Accept—then act. Whatever the present moment contains, accept it as if you had chosen it. Always work with it, not against it. Make it your friend and ally, not your enemy. This will miraculously transform your whole life."

Your life is a fresh chalkboard, a clean slate, a blank canvas. Free yourself from the shackles of regret and move toward your brilliant future.

Are You Missing Out on Life?

I will give you a personal example of how I lost my number one fear in the world: the fear of speaking in public. I didn't have any training or experience with public speaking, so it was something that, in the beginning, scared me.

In a seminar, we were asked to stand in front of the group and sing a capella, without music. My whole body shook. I was sweating. I couldn't even remember the words of my childhood songs. But once I did it, once I sang through the fear, I was never afraid to be in front of people again.

So what happened to create that profound change in my life? First, I had to get out of my comfort zone. Second, I made a decision that affected every other decision for the rest of my life. Please know we are always making decisions, but many times unconsciously. My decision was to give public speaking a try. I reasoned that, if I were able to sing in front of a group without music, speaking in public would be easy. That decision opened a lot of doors for me and especially the door to my willingness to be myself in front of people. I faced my number one fear in the world, the fear of public speaking!

Some studies say that, on a list of things people fear most, death is number two. This is so sad because fearing death we miss out on enjoying life. If we knew who we were, we wouldn't be afraid. While I was writing this book, I had the opportunity to spend two precious days with my mother before she passed. We had talked about death many times and she had attended many of my seminars. This time, I was shocked by how clear she was about it.

She called some of her friends from the hospital and said, "I have finished my work here on earth. I need to go. Please stop thinking I will get better, because it is holding me back."

When some of my nieces or nephew cried, she told them, "This is not good for me. Please realize you don't have to cry for me; I will be even closer to you when I go."

At night, I stayed with my mother. She was having visions and communicating with loved ones who had passed before; we had the most profound conversations about forgiveness and more. I realized in those two days what an amazing person she was. I was able to appreciate her in a completely new way. I am grateful to her for my life and everything she taught me. I am who I am because of her. And now I am most grateful, for she showed me that death is not something to be afraid of, that we are here temporarily and it doesn't end here.

Being aware of death can change our relationship with both death *and* life, and how we relate to each other. Death can actually enrich our lives and help us with our experiences and preconceptions. Death should be present in our life moment to moment since it is a great teacher.

You understand now why it is important to let go of our fears and regrets to start living? We are missing out on life!

We are constantly making decisions, and most of the time our subconscious mind is the one making them for us. Even when we decide to do nothing, we are choosing! So then, if we must choose, why not choose to let go of the fears and set ourselves free? Why don't we choose life instead of death? The Universe is always pushing us and giving us opportunities to expand and grow, but we have free choice. Please know, everything that shows up in your life is always something you are capable of doing. That's why it is showing up in your life!

Memories play in the subconscious, and it is your Inner Child that holds those memories. If I get angry with my Inner Child and reprimand her for being afraid, she will become even more afraid. So, we must show understanding and compassion toward our Inner Child. We should reassure our Inner Child by saying (mentally) that we are by his/her side and will never abandon him/her. We must comfort our

Inner Child (subconscious mind) so he/she will not instigate more fear.

When you think of fear, remember the acronym F.E.A.R., which stands for Face Everything and Rise! This is what life is all about. Of course, in order to be freer and happier, you must leave your comfort zone, feel the fears that come up and choose to keep going. Don't let the fear of not being good enough stop you. If our view of life and existence is more complete, more expanded, if we *know* who we are, it becomes easier to trust, easier to realize that in reality there is nothing to fear, and we can trust and move forward.

We trust that the sun will rise each morning. We trust electronic banking systems and that we will have access to our money. We trust that those we love will treat us a certain way. We trust that the food we're served at a restaurant is in good condition and free of poison. We trust that other drivers will pay attention while driving. The list is endless! Of course, it's wise to be alert to surprises, but without a foundation of trust, living would be unbearable. We would remain locked up in our rooms, victimized by our internal paranoia.

So we don't need to learn how to trust. We already know how to do it. All we need is to take an extra little step and apply that trust to the areas in our lives that challenge us. This trust will help us grow and expand. Life will continuously conspire to bring us experiences of wellbeing. Nothing to worry about! Talk to the "boss"—Spirit, Consciousness, Universe, Source, Creator, God, call it what you'd like—and ask for guidance. That Consciousness is your consciousness, so go ahead and trust! Intellect cannot give you the key to that trust, but your heart, which knows better, will surely provide it.

Zero Frequency® makes it easier to deal with fear. Fears are memories and, as Krishnamurti said, they are not real. And, as with every memory, all you need to do is say *Thank you* and let it go instead of allowing it to take control.

Connect to ZERO *frequency*

Are you living in hell or heaven? Your answer depends on if you let go or not. Moment by moment you are choosing. Will you stay in the prison of your mind, letting past events and negative thoughts control your happiness and decide your fate? Will you keep defending your point of view? Or will you reclaim your power through awareness and letting go?

Here are some ways to connect to Zero Frequency® through the practice of letting go:

1. Deepak Chopra recommends we commit daily to practicing detachment—in all aspects of life. This will help you to stay open to possibilities. How do you practice detachment? One way is to refrain from sharing your opinions with others. Be yourself and allow others to be themselves. Another way is to detach from expectations. When you start to have an expectation, don't engage. Just repeat mentally, "Thank you, but I'm not buying."

2. A fun way of letting go is to laugh at yourself. Laughter helps you let go. HA is the perfect breath. If you can't laugh, just say "HA, HA, HA, HA!" If you are breathing, you are present. You cannot breathe in the past or in the future. Another way to let go is to say, "I am not buying." Don't allow your worries and fears to control you. When you don't resist them, they disappear. Laughing at yourself and your problems and expressing gratitude will bring you back to the present. If you are present, you are pleasant. This may not sound logical or scientific, but aren't you tired of trying logical

things and finding yourself unhappy and stuck? Believe me, the illogical really works. Try it.

3. Remember, negativity is replayed memories from your own beliefs or thoughts or from other people showing up with what looks like their memories and thoughts. Your body stores them, and that, in turn, causes a shift in your energy. Don't take things personally. Just let the negativity pass through you.

4. In Chapter 3, I shared a story about Dr. Jill Bolte Taylor, who wrote about her experience coming back to herself after having a massive stroke. In her book, *My Stroke of Insight*, Bolte Taylor writes about training her brain to be a conscious observer. "When my brain runs loops that feel harshly judgmental, counter-productive, or out of control, I wait ninety seconds for the emotional/physiological response to dissipate and then I speak to my brain as though it is a group of children. I say with sincerity, 'I appreciate your ability to think thoughts and feel emotions, but I am really not interested in thinking these thoughts or feeling these emotions anymore. Please stop bringing this stuff up.'" Essentially, you can do the same thing Bolte Taylor advises us to do: "Consciously ask

your brain to stop looking into specific thought patterns."

5. Surrender. Become humble. Override your thoughts and feelings repeating mentally: "I let go and let God," or, "I let go and trust."

6. Make a list of everything you want to let go and then burn it. Let go to the past what is not working in your life. Let go even of the blaming and complaining. Make more room for Inspiration to come into your life.

7. Regret could be your greatest teacher. Use it as your motivator. Now you know you can do it. Pay attention to your heart. Relax into your heart. Trust your feelings. Do what feels right in your heart. Let go of your mind.

8. Death is what gives meaning to life. Think about it often to make sure your priorities are in the right order. And, if you are worrying about something or if you are mad at someone, ask yourself, "Would I be this worried or this angry if I knew I was going to die today?" Would I worry and be this negative or consider the situation so important if my time was limited? Would I give my attention to the situation or person that is bothering me if I knew that person will die today?

9. Once I visited a school for children with developmental challenges in Budapest. While I stood with the teachers, one of the students approached us and told us she was nervous about participating in an upcoming school play. I asked the teachers to ask the child if I could hug her. She agreed, and, after we all hugged, I asked, "How are you feeling now?" She said she was feeling just fine; the fear had disappeared. Can you believe a simple hug can transform how you feel? Please hug more and definitely include hugging yourself. Hug someone every day and make a commitment to hug a stranger once in a while, but don't forget to ask their permission before you do. You may never know how many lives a hug and a warm smile could save.

You can find more resources on how to go back to Zero Frequency® at *www.zerofrequency.com/bookresources*

Chapter 9

Practice Peace

*That peace which is within us, we must experience
it. And if we are searching for peace outside
we will never find the peace within.*
Prem Rawat

The first Ho'oponopono presentation I ever gave in a prison was at a women's detention center in Mexico City. When I walked into the room where I would speak, I was surprised to see at least seventy women in attendance. The event was not mandatory; all of them had chosen to be there. I was a little nervous. I was sure they were thinking, "What does this woman think she knows?" They had no idea who I was, no reason to trust me and no idea why they should bother to learn about the ancient Hawaiian art of problem solving.

As I shared in Chapter 2, I never write down what I'm going to say before I give a training or a talk. Inspiration flows better when I am spontaneous, and my message serves better that way. The audience receives what they need in that moment. This time, immediately, I had the impression that I was not speaking at a women's prison, but at a women's *conference*. The first words that came out of my mouth were, "You know, this is a spiritual retreat. What are you going to do with your time now?"

Suddenly, I felt all eyes on me. Clearly, the women had not expected me to say *that*.

"Here, you don't have to cook," I continued. "You don't have to go to the supermarket or do a lot of things you used to do. So what are you going to do?"

As I looked out at their expectant faces, I wondered if they had ever considered this question before. Had anyone ever asked?

"This is your time to connect with God and to find God inside of you," I said. "This is your time to realize who you are."

I spoke about the possibilities this place could offer them and about what they could do with their time. They could write about their experiences, about their inspirations and about the things they realize about life now. "It wouldn't be the first time a bestseller came from somebody in jail."

Throughout the talk, I presented a different way of looking at their circumstances. For example, a woman held her infant son, and somehow I knew what she was thinking. To her I said, "You feel sorry for the baby. 'What a poor thing to be born in jail,' you think. But look at this soul choosing this experience. Do you see how many mothers, and aunts and grandmas he created to take care of him?"

When I shared some fables and parables with them, I noticed they looked at each other as if they recognized them. I said, "Oh, you know these stories! These are the things you need to talk about here, not the past and not what brought you here. Stay present."

I pointed at the windows and said, "Those of us outside of these walls think we are free, but we are not free at all, because the worst wars are inside of us. Our thoughts and our worries become our mind's prison. Outside, there is too much noise, and we cannot really connect with ourselves. Here, you can."

At one point in my talk, I looked up and saw a bird's nest. Somehow, the birds had come through a high window in the room and built a nest in the rafters. "You think you are not trustworthy," I said to the women. "Look. The birds trust you and they know. They trust you enough to make their nest here." Their faces lit up and some sat taller in their chairs.

After I finished, most of the women came up to me and hugged me, thanked me and blessed me. I was shocked to receive such a reaction. When I do this work, I always get emotional, because I am still amazed that God trusts me enough to put me in front of these people and do this kind of work. I am always so grateful.

That night, the person who arranged for me to speak at the women's prison received an update. They said, "Usually, the jail is so loud at night. There are always fights and screaming. But tonight, the jail was so quiet, we went down to check if the prisoners had escaped!"

I share this story to show you that peace is possible, even in an imperfect world. When we have peace in our minds, we have peace in our lives. And when we have peace in our lives, there is more peace in the lives of those around us. The peace carries forward, and forward still, until it touches every corner of the earth. This is how we co-create a peaceful world.

For me, a perfect world would be one in which we all do what we love, expressing our unique talents when interacting with others. We would all definitely have money, and no one would be thinking about killing, engaging in war or taking advantage of others. When we are successful, when we are happy, we have more peace in our lives, and thus there is more peace in the lives of those around us.

The world may not yet be perfect. The prisons may be full, the wars rage on and the poor struggle to find food and shelter. However, we can change the world. If we can create a quiet night in a prison that was always full of noise and fighting, we can end war and poverty and we can stop taking advantage of others. We can practice peace. It begins with us.

Peace Is Outside Our Comfort Zone

A year after my presentation at the women's prison, I returned to Mexico to give a series of talks. I was looking forward to continuing visiting and working with the women, but when I attempted to go back, I was shocked to learn that the prison authorities didn't want me to work with the women anymore. Their argument was that the inmates were "too quiet." I found this difficult to believe. Their decision made no sense!

On that same trip, I gave a talk at a preschool where all the teachers had come to my seminars and were my students. The kids were behaving so well that it caught my attention. I could feel the peace and happiness in the air. It was right then that the parents found out that the teachers were practicing my teachings and offering them to the children.

During my talk with the parents, a mother shared that her son kept repeating, "Thank you, Mommy!" and, "I'm sorry, Mommy." He was constantly saying "Sorry" or "Thank you" under his breath. His mother didn't know where that behavior was coming from, because he evidently did not learn it from her.

Another mother said that she had noticed a change in her daughter's attitude. Before coming to this preschool, the little girl had always fought with her cousin over a toy they both wanted to play with, and now the girl showed respect and acceptance and was more generous toward her cousin. It was as if the girl realized the toy was not worth fighting or arguing over.

I was so pleased to see the impact of letting go on little hearts and minds. Suddenly, I had a realization.

I asked the mothers, "Isn't it true that when your children are too quiet, you go and check up on them to see what they are doing, because you are sure they are doing something bad?"

Aha! Now I understood why the authorities no longer wanted me to work at the women's prison—they didn't trust the quiet.

We don't trust peace. It makes us feel uneasy. Peace takes us out of our comfort zone, and we don't know how to behave appropriately. In a way, we think that if someone is peaceful then something bad is surely going to happen... or has already happened.

Later that year, when I presented at a seminar for adult students, I asked them, "Are you really sure that you are looking for peace?"

You may say you want peace, but then you sabotage it by not trusting it, which is the opposite of what peace requires. It is very important that you become aware of this tendency in all humans and in you. We need to stop being suspicious of peace.

So, now, I ask you: Are you really sure that you are looking for peace?

We Can Each Make a Difference

In this book, we have paved the easiest way to achieve a perfect world. You have the power to change your future and the future of humanity. You only have to take one hundred percent responsibility for the memories that are playing inside you and press the delete key to let go of the ones that make your life toxic and miserable so you can make a difference in the world. Now you have the right passwords to do it: *Thank you* and *I love you. The things I could be grateful for... This will also pass. I let go and trust. I am not going to worry. Go with the flow.* You know the words that work for you, that bring you back to present and into the Zero Frequency® flow. Even if you don't feel it or mean it, saying these words will do the trick. As you do this, you are choosing to let go and let God do the work.

Our beliefs, opinions and judgments enslave us, and we need to work together to free ourselves from them. The way is to teach by example, so we inspire others to do the same. In this way we expand and create a pandemic of love and peace. Remember, love and peace are contagious and can cure anything.

We will not convince others with words. There is nothing to convince, because everyone has their beliefs, and some of our ideas will always be rebutted.

Choose peace. Choose happiness. Choose to be different, even if people think your unconventional ways are crazy.

You are your own rescue. Do not wait. Life is a game, and you have to be willing to get on the field and play it. Don't be a spectator. What is called for is having the right energy and being a good example. Practicing Zero Frequency® allows this vibrational energy to be achieved, and it is contagious! We can decide what wars are not worth fighting, because we know it's not good for us. Not only do they not bring the results we expect, wars do a lot of harm to the Earth and to humanity. Ending war requires the courage to take on an "impossible" mission. You are a miracle and you have to play big. You have to stop relying on the sixteen bits of information most of us use and start using the eleven million bits of information available to you. I'm not saying it's easy. Some of your painful memories are strong and stubborn. You have to be serious, keep letting them go, and stay conscious. You need to believe in yourself.

Pope Francis said, "Peacemaking calls for courage, much more so than warfare. It calls for the courage to say yes to encounter and no to conflict; yes to dialogue and no to violence."

We cannot do it alone. We must have the humility to recognize that we need to work in alliance with the Universe. This alliance is the source of the solution to all our problems.

Everyone Can Learn Peace

It's wonderful to witness how children can get to Zero Frequency® so easily and how their attitudes change almost immediately. In the preschool in Mexico, they implemented a practice to promote gratitude. Every day, from 11:00 a.m. to 11:10 a.m., they practice "gratitude time." The children are invited to come to the microphone and share something they are grateful for. The teachers told me that sometimes the kids say thank you even to a fly that passes by. Amazing!

In Mexico, I also had the chance to give presentations at Kadima, a Jewish institution that helps both children and adults with autism and Down syndrome, as well as in a psychiatric hospital. In both places the same comment was made: "How was it possible that the participants kept so quiet, behaved so well and stayed through the whole presentation?" The directors and caretakers couldn't believe it. In the psychiatric hospital, one inmate was known to always scream very loudly, but during my presentation he kept quiet the whole time. I say *Thank you, God*, for having this effect, even on these special people.

In both Kadima and the psychiatric hospital, I asked the participants to share at the end of my presentation. Those who shared were the most "special" ones. It was so moving to see how they gave thanks for the presentation.

The people in the psychiatric hospital and in Kadima took the opportunity to thank their families and the people who took care of them. They thanked life itself. It was amazing to witness this in people who, theoretically, have challenging problems.

One girl at Kadima was sitting upfront and wanted to talk and make comments all the time, even when I played a video. She insisted on knowing what the video was about. She had no patience. I realized how that happens to all of us all the time. We don't live in the moment. We want to anticipate the result. I explained to her, "Tomorrow is not important. Only the present moment, only our experience in the now, at Zero, is important." She listened and she got it. And from that moment on, she was quiet and peaceful.

Finally, during that same trip, I gave a presentation at Mexico Sonríe, a foundation that assists children with cancer and their families. Once again, I was humbled to present and give people hope. I gave them tools and helped them see that everything is perfect, that they can start to see people and situations how God sees them, and not how they, and all of us, see them (through our memories, opinions and judgments). I reminded them that God does not create anything that is not perfect. This awareness is something we can all live by and give credit to ourselves for understanding it.

The Role of Women in World Peace

In a training I presented in Hungary, a woman asked me, "Why are there always more women than men in these kinds of trainings?"

I asked her, "Who are the people who don't let go, who don't forget and who remember every bad or sad moment of the past? Yes, we women. This is why we need more training to remember how to let go and not take things personally and to stay more present."

When we talk world peace, we need to stress the importance of women's role for many reasons. Women are more connected to their feelings and could be more open, flexible and understanding. We influence our children since we spend more time with them. We need to set an example. Our children observe our attitudes and behaviors more than they listen to our words.

As women we need to wake up, find out who we are, regain our power and trust our own Inspiration. Women know things, even though they cannot always explain how they know them. It is time to start trusting this knowing. Women are not as weak as society has made us believe. Please, I am not putting men down in any way, and I don't suggest women need to compete with men. It is about complementing each other, realizing that we have different talents and ways of thinking and doing things—not better, nor worse, but essential differences that must be honored if we are to attract more peace into our lives. And from there, it will be easier for peace to spread in the world.

Women, men and young ones, can join my world peace campaign *Peace within Is World Peace,* whose motto is "Peace begins with me." You can find it at *www.PeaceWithinIsWorldPeace.com.*

We Are All One Big Family

I had an incredible learning experience during a training I gave in Bristol, United Kingdom. The person who organized the training was a big Muslim guy from Ghana. He picked me up at the airport, and on the way to the hotel I was shocked when he asked, "You have a Christian background, don't you?"

Well, you can guess what my response was: "No, I am Jewish."

He mentioned that many of his Muslims friends were coming to the training. We agreed to meet later and talk about what I could and couldn't say, and I was a little bit nervous about that because I am always myself and very spontaneous during trainings. As I said before, I don't prepare and I don't think. It is important for me to go with the flow and always come from Inspiration.

In our meeting with the local organizers that afternoon, as we were going through the dos and don'ts, I said, "I want you to know that I am going to say what God wants me to say!"

During the training, the Muslims were open, flexible and happy to hear what I had to say. My only protester was a religious Christian lady who initially challenged me about everything I said and questioned where my information was coming from. As the training progressed and we were letting go of our painful memories, her attitude toward me changed.

She started finding correlations between what I was saying and teachings she knew from Christian scriptures and recited passages from the Bible to prove it.

The class ended up being a fun "competition" between Zero Frequency®, the Koran and the Bible. We had a great time finding the commonalities in everybody's religious backgrounds and how the different scriptures were actually saying the same thing. It was such a wonderful confirmation of what I was finding in my travels—that we are all family. We need to do more letting go, keep our mouths shut and *listen*.

We Are Talking About the Same Thing

On my travels, I've been given so many opportunities to practice peace and to witness peace. During a weekend seminar I gave in Chile, a Palestinian man came up to me and said, "When I saw your Jewish last name, I thought, 'What will she have to teach me?' I was right. I don't agree with anything you taught us today."

He then told me everything he believed. When he finished, to his surprise, I told him I agreed with everything he said.

"Please be open and flexible, because I think we may be using different words for the same beliefs and ideas."

The man returned to the seminar the next day and excitedly shared a story with the class about an encounter he had with the police the previous night. "I repeated 'I love you,' the tool you gave me yesterday, and, just like that, the situation was resolved!" He was so amazed at the incredible results he achieved that, at the end of the class, he gave me a big hug and exclaimed, "This is peace in the Middle East!"

This story is important because it demonstrates that when we let go of trying to convince others of our point of view, we stay at Zero Frequency®. At Zero, we have a different attitude and a different perception. When people feel accepted and respected, suddenly peace unfolds. When we try to over explain and convince, the exact opposite occurs.

I am not saying that it is easy to let go in the middle of a tense dialogue. The previous day, when the Palestinian man was saying that he disagreed with everything I was teaching, my intellect kicked in, telling me, "Return him the money and ask him to leave." Instead I chose to let go and not permit my opinions and judgments to take over. Since I did not allow the chatter of the ego to determine my reaction, I was able to be present and really listen to him. That's how I realized that we were talking about the same thing but calling it different names. I was able to exercise active listening, which consists of being so present and attentive that you begin to empathize with the person and understand their motivations.

When you relinquish the need to be right, you suddenly know things or you come up with unexpected ideas or solutions to problems, not knowing where you got them. This way, it is more likely that the response you offer will not feed the tension, but, on the contrary, will dissipate it.

We Need to Change and Forgive

This point is essential. If we want peace in the world, it is imperative that we begin accepting other people's perspectives. We must realize that others do not see things the same way we do. This awareness allows me to accept myself just the way I am and do what is right for me. Being fully myself helps me accept other people being fully themselves. It helps me accept our differences. The root of disrespect for others is disrespect for oneself.

If we don't believe in ourselves, we cannot respect others. We constantly feel the need to defend our point of view, we take things personally, we interpret a difference of opinion as being attacked. Hence the need to have others see exactly as we see and feel. This is precisely the origin of all wars.

When I present in Israel, because I am Jewish I can tell the audience things I could not tell them if I were a Gentile. They would get offended. What am I telling them? That if we do not change and act differently, we cannot expect the same from others. That if we are not going to forgive, if we continue to see ourselves as victims, we will not end this long-lasting conflict between Israelis and Palestinians.

Someone has to take responsibility and say, "I am sorry for whatever is in me that attracts this hatred." Obviously, this "something" that attracts hatred is memories—the memories that tell us that it is the other who is to blame; that it is they who have to change; that we are perfect! These memories even tell us that we are the chosen ones! Now, who is going to turn on the light? Who will take responsibility for the replayed painful memories? Someone has to turn on that light. And when someone turns it on, it will turn on for everybody. The light does not discriminate.

Haven't you noticed that the sun shines on everybody? This is the only way to bring peace! See, most of those memories come from our ancestors and have been ingrained in us for generations. Those past wars have nothing to do with what is going on right now. They are just memories we inherited.

Where Is the Solution?

At a training I gave in Hungary, a woman who comes to all my trainings there raised her hand and asked me if it was okay to go to peace demonstrations. I asked her, "In the past, have you noticed that demonstrations worked? Do they bring the answers or produce the results you are looking for?"

She responded, "Not really."

Then I said, "Then, you can go, but if you do, be sure to take one hundred percent responsibility, press the delete key and allow God to erase."

We have to realize that the solutions are not on this plane. Stop thinking, discussing and manipulating! We need to realize that a more intelligent mind than ours exists. As I shared earlier, it's the wisdom that thought up the human body, the oceans and the flowers. I call it God. Call it what you wish, but you need to realize there is a more intelligent mind that can come up with much better solutions than our intellect.

The Jews have many stories of miracles in their ancestral history. How could it be that they won wars when they were so few and had hardly any weapons? Could it be that it was because they were believers? They had no education, but they knew to let go and let God. They believed. They trusted! They asked for help and guidance and they received help from the forces of the Universe. They didn't do it alone.

This is the only way to bring peace in the world. The solutions to *all* our problems come from Spirit. But we keep looking in the wrong places and asking the wrong questions. All the problems we have, including the shortage of food and water, are already solved. Only power groups with their vested interests and need to control and manipulate slow down the process of finding them. All the solutions humanity has ever needed, all the innovative ideas that evolved the world, have always come from scientists who were open to receive them by Inspiration. And thankfully more and more such scientists continue to emerge.

So we need to become humble, stop the thinking (intellect) and live at Zero (present). Being conscious and aware, open and flexible, is essential as we face our challenges and do our best to bring peace to the world. Zero Frequency® is the missing piece in the puzzle.

Connect to ZERO frequency

If we are to obtain peace in a world where violence and hate exist, we must find inner peace. When we find inner peace, we will be able to spread world peace. Through consciousness, everything is possible. To be agents of peace, we must have a peaceful heart. Here are some ways you can connect to Zero Frequency® through practicing peace:

1. Listen attentively. Tell your judgements, "Thank you, but no thank you," and stay present. When you truly listen to others without assumption or judgment, you are better able to hear their points of view and offer them compassion. You are also better able to hear and see their true selves and intentions. This is the pathway to peace.

2. Stop the excuses and the blame games. Stop judging people and indulging in feeling that you are better than others. When you feel the urge to keep score, think of things you admire and appreciate in that person.

3. Remember, you are not owed anything. When you view others as having more than you, when you feel the Universe has short-changed you, count your blessings. Remind yourself: "I can do it. I have everything I need inside me. The Universe is right there supporting me every step of the way."

4. Live life as if this day is all you have and treat others as if the same is true for them. When you live this way, it is easy to forgive and let go and to make peace with yourself and others. Do not leave forgiveness for tomorrow.

5. Reflect on the people who have had the greatest influence in your life and why. Recall the moments when you received an unexpected kindness or offer of compassion. Remember some words you read or places and activities that had a positive impact on your life.

6. In the Arbinger Institute's 2009 book, *Leadership and Self-Deception: Getting Out of the Box,* self-deception is described as a "box" that we live in, unaware. One way to get out of the box is to change your vibration by enjoying something you love, such as music that inspires you and connects you with your real essence.

7. If you want to bring more peace into your life and have more peaceful relationships, take responsibility and stop blaming and complaining. Realize that there is something in you attracting the problem. You created it; you can change it!

You can find more resources on how to go back to Zero Frequency® at *www.zerofrequency.com/bookresources*

Chapter 10

Practice Abundance

Real riches are the riches possessed inside.
B. C. Forbes

We all want abundance. In our search for a more abundant life, we take classes, read books, listen to lectures. And yet, we reject anything simple. We are so programmed for unhappiness that we find happiness suspicious. We are so programmed for lack that we treat abundance as suspicious. If we see someone who is not worried, we call them "irresponsible." If we see someone happy, we think the person is "up to something." And yet, being happy and content is not only easy; it is born of taking full responsibility. I shared more about this with you earlier.

And being happy and content is living in abundance. This is our natural condition. Our biggest dreams and our deepest desires are simple to fulfill when we are at Zero Frequency®.

Someone once asked me how I defined success. For me, success has to do with being able to be happy for no particular reason. A happy person is already successful, because they are happy without attachments and expectations. Our goal should be to be able to get up in the morning and feel at peace, no matter what problems we may have. It's not about seeking the perfect life in which there are no problems. What we have to look for is a way to recognize problems as opportunities the Universe gives us so that we can get to know ourselves, grow and set ourselves free.

The ability to be happy and at peace for no reason brings opportunities, abundance and doors that begin to open. Before I began practicing Ho'oponopono, I did not believe any of these ideas. I used to think that more money came to people who already had money *and* that you had to work hard for the money. But I started noticing that people who had money didn't think or worry about it. Most of us, even when we have money, do exactly the opposite, and in so doing we stop the natural flow of money. Once I understood this, I started telling my teenage children that their job was to be happy. I told them to watch how good things came to happy people, how they seemed to be "lucky."

We should not expect to be successful—as our families or society define it. First on our list should be to be happy. Albert Schweitzer said, "Success is not the key to happiness. Happiness is the key to success. If you love what you do, you will succeed." When you are happy, you are yourself and you are in the flow. That flow takes you to the right place, at the perfect time, with the right people. Suddenly you are "lucky." Everything begins to work for you, and you find the time, energy and—and even more importantly—the will to do whatever you need to do. When you are happy, you are at Zero Frequency®. You stop being an obstacle in your own life because you no longer react emotionally. You are present, free and open, and everything comes to you easily. Living in abundance starts with being ourselves. Everything comes because we are at peace, because we are happy for no particular reason.

Do you want to be successful and become a millionaire in order to feel better or to be admired by others? Do you do it to prove yourself? If you do it for any of those reasons, it will be very hard to attract the wealth you desire. Money may come and go. I hope you do your work because you love it, because you want to contribute, or because you have a purpose. Then attracting wealth will come effortlessly.

In his book *The World's Greatest Salesman*, Og Mandino says: "Money, my son, should never be your goal in life. True wealth is of the heart, not of the purse... No, my son, do not aspire for wealth and labor only to be rich. Strive instead for happiness, to be loved and to love and most important to acquire peace of mind and serenity."

Whatever you do, whether for financial gain, as a volunteer or when it's your own artistic or scientific project, you have to give it your best. Even if, right now, you are not yet satisfied with what you do, still do your best. The Universe is watching. The raise, new position, business opportunity or creative insight will not come from where you think it is going to come from. And it will surprise you!

Do not waste your time waiting for money to bring you the joy you seek. There isn't enough money in the world that can make you happy; there are no new cars or houses big enough to make you happy. So are you going to keep looking out there? It is time to wake up and become aware. Time to make better choices. The possibility of changing your life is in your hands. And of course, in your thoughts.

Live every moment at its fullest. All moments fully lived are themselves an expression of success. Achieving success is not a finish line. Anyone hoping to achieve a future goal lives under a lot of tension and distress. Such hope destroys people's lives. They do not realize that the ultimate goal should be to live in the here and now. Forget about success and seek happiness. Do the things that make you feel good. Always follow your heart and you will live in abundance—you will have all that you need and more.

Success or Failure?

Remember I told you about my TV show? I want to share another story with you about that experience. Producing a show for television requires a lot of money, time and effort. I could have bought a house—with cash!—with the money I spent on my show.

One day, I told God, "If I have to do the TV show again, I will do it, but I need a sign. I need confirmation." Next I gave God an idea about how to give me that sign. I said, "God, if I'm not supposed to do the show, I shouldn't get the contract from the

TV station. If I get it, I will sign it, so if you don't want me to sign the contract, do something so that I never get it."

The next day, my teacher, Dr. Ihaleakalá, called me and said, "I need to talk to you. I want you to know that I was not thinking of you or your TV show, but when I was meditating, I heard Divinity say very clearly to me, 'Tell Mabel it's okay to do the TV show.'"

I was really shocked. God had found a better and clearer sign than I had expected.

Because I got the okay, my sign from the Universe, I went all in with the production. We rented a mansion in Los Angeles and we created an amazing daily show. Along the way, my producer kept asking me if I understood what I was getting into. I kept telling him, "Yes. We have God on our side."

After all of our hard work and hundreds of thousands of dollars invested, I presented the project to many sponsors who had expressed interest. Nobody signed. Nobody gave us any money. A month passed, and I kept paying the bills. Not one penny came in from any source. So, I asked Dr. Ihaleakalá to meditate and check if I had been doing something wrong. He meditated and asked and then told me that he heard that I had completed what I needed to do spiritually and I could quit the show right away.

That is when my intellect took over. "What?" I said. "Leave the show now? After all of the money I invested? No way. I am sure we will close some sponsorship deals now and the money will start coming in any minute."

I kept going another month. I kept paying, and still no money came in. Except this time, it wasn't my savings I was spending. It was borrowed money, and I ended up in debt. Eventually, I stopped waiting, and paying, and trying. I acknowledged that the reason I was instructed to do the TV show was because I had a *spiritual debt to pay*. Sometimes, we move forward with a project or an idea expecting the only outcome is the positive result we label "success," and yet, the important part was *the experience and the opportunity to make amends.*

Can you see that Divinity finds the way to communicate with all of us? Whether you ask for a sign or you meditate and listen for the answer, God will answer. The key is, you have to listen even when it doesn't make sense to you, and especially when you would prefer a different answer. If I would have listened to God's message as he told it to Dr. Ihaleakalá and quit my TV show in the first month, I might not have ended up in debt.

Because we follow guidance and do what is spiritually correct, that doesn't mean it will always be easy. It *does* mean that it will be perfect for you, and it will give you the opportunity to make corrections. We don't always realize or understand how an experience can serve us on our journey. The many times we complain, or think we've failed or lost, or when we think things are unfair, we are not acknowledging that *everything is perfect.* We think we've lost, but we've actually won a lot.

Practicing abundance does not mean you will never experience failure. It simply means that you stay open to all blessings, even those given to us in disguise.

Let me tell you that right after those two months, invitations started coming—and never stopped coming—to present seminars in many different parts of the world. Many contracts were signed. This reminds me of when I started promoting and organizing the Ho'oponopono seminars for my teacher back in 1998. He called and said, "I don't know if you are going to make money organizing the trainings, but I can assure you, the money will come from somewhere."

Something I learned very early in my path with him is about helping others and money. The first time he came to Los Angeles for an event I was organizing, I mentioned to him that many people wanted to come to the training but they couldn't afford it. This was his answer: "You can do whatever you want, but please know that when you help somebody to cross the river, they not only miss the opportunity to learn everything they would have learned if they had crossed that river by themselves, *you* collect more rocks in your backpack, more things to correct, because it was not right to help in the first place."

To create anything sustainable in your life—relationships, artistic expression, innovative business, service to society—from the state of mind of being at Zero Frequency®, you must get rid at once of the idea of easy and hard or success and failure. This means letting go of the anxiety of success (future) and the fear of failure (past).

This view is fully shared by Osho, who states that we will inevitably bear the thought of failure if we are thinking about success. According to him, if we think of success, we will not get it, because we will be projected into the future instead of being fully present with our work. In this projection into the future there will be greed, ambition and ego. We will also experience fear—the fear of not getting what we want—the fear of failure. Osho takes this phrase from Lu-Tsu: "Work quietly, silently, un-troubled by any idea of success or failure." And he concludes, "Do not look too far forward; otherwise you will miss the next step. Success comes by itself. Leave it alone… If your work is headed in the right direction, with the appropriate effort, with your whole being on it, the reward follows automatically."

We forget Osho's advice when we look for quick fixes and financial windfalls. When we chase success rather than let it come by itself, we are not operating from an abundant mindset. If we are lucky and success comes anyway, we won't be prepared for the reality. This is why many lottery winners declare bankruptcy three to five years after winning.[*] They are still living with and making decisions from a lack mindset, which becomes self-fulfilling.

Don't define yourself by your circumstances. Be willing to take risks, give yourself as many chances as possible. Open your mind and take one step at a time. Do one simple and easy thing you know you can do.

---

[*] «The Financial Consequences of Winning the Lottery», Hankins, Scott; Hoekstra, Mark; Skiba, Paige Marta. *The Review of Economic and Statistics*, vol. 93, Issue 3, agosto de 2011, pp. 961-969.

You need to be okay to live with failures, mistakes, defeats, rejections and not take them personally. Let go of the fear of failure. Be willing to feel the fear and do it anyway. I love the way Og Mandino says it: "Never feel shame for trying and failing for he who has never failed is he who has never tried. Failure will never overtake you if your determination to succeed is strong enough."

When you practice abundance, you won't experience setbacks or detours as failures. We may not always understand why something didn't work out, but with an abundant mindset, we know that ultimately whatever happens is for our greater good— and the good of humanity.

Passion Is Your True North

Sometimes the problem is that we don't know what we want. So no matter what happens, we will always feel unhappy. Maybe what is right and perfect and will make us infinitely happy is in front of us, but we don't recognize it because we're always looking "out there," comparing and focusing on what we think we lack. This is why it is fundamental that we trust ourselves and our talents. If we dare to be ourselves and do what we are passionate about, what we love to do, what makes us happy, we will have the compass in our hands and we will never lose our path. This compass connects us with Zero Frequency® and always brings us back to ourselves; it is our own true north.

If you don't know what you would do if money were not an issue, just keep an open mind, and you will be able to recognize your path when it presents itself before you. When opportunity shows up, have complete certainty that things will work out. Don't be afraid to commit and do what you need to do. Be open to different and new approaches. Put passion first and money last. If you love and enjoy what you do, you will automatically and naturally attract the money and resources you need to accomplish your heart's desire.

Stay conscious, flexible, vigilant and focused. New paths may open up, and you don't want to miss them. Your commitment to your heart's desire will support you in preventing distractions from taking you off your course. Sometimes it will take some "work," but remember, when you do what you love, you cannot call it work. When you do what you love, you are not conscious of the passage of time; you're not looking at your watch anxiously waiting for the time to go home, or shut the manuscript on your desk or put away your paintbrushes and canvases. You are having fun doing it. You are happy!

Understanding why we do the things we do will help us to do the "required work" of life, the tasks and actions that, although tedious or challenging, will help us live our passion. When you align your passion with the work required to experience it, you won't procrastinate. During a conference I gave in Bogota, a mother raised her hand and said, "Mabel, we have to discipline our children. For example, my son brought a bad grade from school, and I told him he couldn't go to the soccer game that weekend."

I told her, "The sooner we learn that our actions have conse-quences, the better. We adults have consequences too. We are where we are as a consequence of our thoughts, deeds, actions and emotions. I wouldn't call it discipline nor rewards and punishments; they are consequences. So I would tell him in advance, 'if you have good grades you go to the soccer game and if you have bad grades you don't. *Either way it's okay.* I will love you no matter what. You will be okay no matter what, but you decide what you want.'"

Then a man raised his hand and told me that the boy who didn't get to go to the soccer game was in the room and asked me to talk to him directly. I told the child, "Listen, I love what I do, but this life comes with a package, and the package includes a lot of tasks I don't like to do. I do them because I know they are part of the package. I understand *why* I am doing them."

"Next time," I continued, "you study, not because you are really interested in what you are studying, but because what you really want is to go to the soccer game."

It is very important to know *why* you do the things you do. When you have a passion for something, then you are more willing to do the part of the package (the process) you need to do to get to where you want to get.

As mentioned earlier, Joseph Campbell said, "Follow your bliss. If you do follow your bliss, you put yourself on a kind of track that has been there all the while waiting for you, and the life you ought to be living is the one you are living. When you can see that, you begin to meet people who are in the field of your bliss, and they open doors to you. I say, follow your bliss. Don't be afraid, and doors will open where you didn't know they were going to be. If you follow your bliss, doors will open for you that wouldn't have opened for anyone else."

The million-dollar idea will come from Inspiration. It will come during a dream or when you're taking a shower or a walk, not when you analyze or make an effort to come up with it. If you choose to follow it, as Campbell said, all of the doors will open for you. So do not engage with your self-doubt and the tiresome thoughts that are putting you down. Be patient. Persist. Don't give up! This is what it means to live at Zero Frequency®—moment by moment, day by day—holding the key to happiness and success in your hand.

Remember, our minds are programmed by our experiences and messages we receive from others and from the media and society. Do you really want money and success? Is the dream you yearn to fulfill really yours or is it borrowed from someone else's story? Has your purpose been forced upon you by a family member? If you are still feeling this way, please re-read Chapter 2: The Journey Back to Yourself. And please, let go and do all you can to connect to Zero.

As is true of all things, finding your purpose is easy. All you must do is what makes you happy. All you must do is follow your bliss, even when the path may not seem clear. Place your hand in God's hand

and keep walking toward what makes you smile, what makes you light up inside. This is your purpose.

Money Follows Love

Often passion gets confused with *ambition*; you should never confuse the two. I consider that successful people are those who value themselves and chase their dreams, not for the sake of money but for the longings of their soul. The ingrained idea that money leads to happiness is one of our civilization's most prevalent false beliefs and misunderstandings. In general, when we ask people what they want to be, they respond they want to be millionaires. That is the wrong objective! If you ask someone who is already a millionaire, they will tell you that their goal had never been the money, but to do more of what they loved. All successful people agreed that they did what they did because they were passionate about it, not because of the money. See? They didn't have a specific goal at all. And yet, the money followed. They trusted, set aside their focus on goals and planning and let go of specific outcomes.

We have learned to work for money, but that's not an adequate, wise or even practical motivation. It neither makes us happy nor provides us with the peace we are seeking. It also doesn't bring us the security we long for. It is essential to realize that you must change the programming that tells you that you must work only for financial gain. The key is to discover your talents and the activities that feed your passion. Make doing work the work you love one of your main goals. If you don't, your chances of failing in business and life will be much higher than your probability of success.

In his book, *Born to Run,* Christopher McDougall relayed a message that helped him as an endurance runner:

"There are two goddesses in your heart," he [a Tarahumara Indian in Mexico] told them. "The Goddess of Wisdom and the Goddess of Wealth. Everyone thinks they need to get wealth first, and wisdom will come. So they concern themselves with chasing money. But they have it backwards. You have to give your heart to the Goddess of Wisdom, give her all your love and attention, and the Goddess of Wealth will become jealous, and follow you."

We become wealthy when we have an abundant mindset and put love first. Money might not pour down on us immediately when we start doing what we love, but, as we persevere and trust, it begins flowing more and more easily. So, if you do what you do to answer your heart's call, you do not need to worry because everything else will come on its own, effortlessly.

When you practice abundance, you become a magnet for all that you could ever need or want.

What Is Your Talent?

If you've ever felt as though you don't have a special talent, or purpose or passion, you're not alone. So many people are searching for something they are good at, something they love. Many believe that they don't have anything special to offer the world and that they will never find their passion. What they don't realize is, they are listening to their intellect.

Your intellect is obsessed with knowing and understanding everything. It wants to verify things, assess risk, determine an idea's viability. To tap into your passion and find your talent, you must trust your heart. In doing this, you stay open to the possibilities, to pursuits that you may not have considered and natural abilities you may not have acknowledged you have. For example, being organized is a talent. You can help others who are disorganized by making their lives easier. Being honest is also a talent, just as knowing how to be a good listener and having a positive attitude are talents.

Once I did an exercise where they asked me to name two of my talents that I used when I interact with others. My answer was my passion and enthusiasm. Would you consider these attributes talents? Perhaps not. And yet, for me, they are. I use my passion and enthusiasm to connect people with their true essence. I didn't think when I answered; the answer came definitely from Inspiration. Of course there are all those other talents, the ones that are more publicly recognized, like having a great singing voice or the stamina and muscles to be a world-class runner, but I wanted to mention a few that are often underestimated and which, when used, can be really helpful in helping others.

And if you also connect to Zero Frequency®, there are no words to describe how much help you can provide! Your contribution will be magnificent and greater than you can ever imagine. Why? Because when you take responsibility and know that people appear in your life to give you a chance to correct whatever is playing in you, whatever gets corrected in you gets also corrected in them. We hold common memories, remember? And so when we change, everybody else changes. The healing goes both ways. Having this awareness, being a therapist, a parent or a professional of any kind becomes much easier and more rewarding.

Do you like to be with people? Do you adore a certain type of product or service? Allow what you love to do and what you are passionate about to be your compass. What you love to do and how you use it in interacting and helping people could be your guiding light in finding your perfect profession.

Sometimes we discover or realize our passion right away. Other times we don't. In the beginning, I didn't think that being a teacher or public speaker could really be my thing until, gradually, I realized that I loved doing it so much that I would have done it even for free! If you are not immediately clear on what your talent is, explore and try different things. Some of them may look like they are your passion, but you find out later that they are not and that's okay. Just keep on trying.

As you search for your talent, you might find yourself doing things that you don't really enjoy and experience these instances as a "failure." But this is not true. The process is like walking through a hallway to find the right room, and each time you must close a door for another one to open. You may have to be patient, but one day your passion will reveal itself in all its glory.

It's important to continue trying and enjoying the process. Be grateful every step of the way. In order to do this, it is best to be patient and humble, acknowledging that you are only taking your first steps. This is easy to do when you practice abundance. In this context, you must let go of your money-related expectations, trust and allow yourself to be guided by what you love and what you are attracted to. Don't think too much.

Many times, a good way to start your journey is by volunteering. I often tell people, "If you like to cook, why don't you volunteer at a restaurant so you can learn, even if you don't get paid?" or, "Start by cooking at home." It wouldn't be the first time someone starts from home and ends up having a chain of restaurants that later becomes a franchise. I started this new teaching career of mine as a hobby, by volunteering.

A good example of this is none other than Albert Einstein. He loved science, but initially science was not his profession. He had a job as a technical assistant at a Swiss patent office. But while he was working there to pay his bills, he wrote four of his most important papers. Sometimes this is the way to start. Sometimes the key is to make time for what we love to do in between our obligatory activities.

When you start searching, the Universe will present you with adequate situations, but you must take the initial step. The first step is making the decision that you really want to find your talent and passion. And you are not going to let your financial burdens stop you. I will tell you again and again, the Universe has the "know how;" it's just waiting for you to take the first step and to trust!

You Are Right Where You Are Supposed to Be... Today

In 2003, I was involved with networking business groups in Los Angeles and traveled to Thailand and Korea with one of them. I still owned my accounting practice and I was working on finishing my first book during the trip.

In the hotel in Seoul, I found a book of the Teachings of the Buddha in the nightstand in my room. I looked at the book and thought, "I would love to read it, but I don't have enough time." I decided to open it randomly and read only that page. Well, what I read was so profound that I included it in my book. Then I noticed that the book had been printed in City of Industry, California, where I had accounting clients and where I would go to meet them once a month. So I thought, next time I go to my clients I will visit this printing place.

At the time we didn't have GPS, and, using my paper maps, the printer was hard to find. When I finally arrived, I noticed it was an industrial site. I decided to go in anyway. Walking in, I saw only one person in this huge place and asked a nonsense question: "Was there a Buddhist temple here before?"

The person looked at me as if I were really crazy. Just then, someone else walked in and, having heard me ask the question, said, "Please come this way." He took me inside to the offices, and there it was: a large library with the books of the Teachings of the Buddha translated into all languages. They were distributing the books to hotels around the world so travelers would find them and take them with them! I found that this company was producing precision instruments such as microscopes in order to financially support their mission of distributing the Teachings of the Buddha.

As I drove back home that day, I understood many things. Many times I had asked myself why I had studied to be an accountant. Was it to generate the resources that would allow me to prepare myself to travel with my teacher? Was it to invest in the TV and radio shows I produced for the Latino community in Los Angeles? I realized that the Universe, in its utmost intelligence, had "arranged" my initial profession as an accountant so I would earn enough money to start on my spiritual path and eventually pursue my mission to be the teacher I am today.

You may not understand the purpose of your current profession or circumstances until later in life. One thing is for sure—when you let go and let the Universe guide you, all will be made clear. When you practice abundance, setting aside all of your programmed beliefs about money, success and achievement, all paths are the right path.

Self-Worth and Trust Are Keys to Success

What do you see when you look at yourself in the mirror? Do you see yourself like a helpless little cat or do you see yourself as a lion that can do anything and knows that everything is possible?

These two things—self-worth and trust—are pivotal in practicing abundance. I, personally, learned to let go and to trust, and God continues to surprise me every time. If we want to manifest our dreams and desires, letting go and trusting will usher in incredible results. When you let go and trust, you will see that God brings you all the resources you need, exactly when you need them, effortlessly.

In 2009, my financial situation changed. A certain stream of income I was counting on suddenly stopped. I already had many employees at that time, and this income was helping me pay their salaries. The first question that came to mind was, "What am I going to do now? Where will I get the money to pay all these people?"

My very smart intellect told me, "You'll have to go back to preparing taxes!"

As soon I started to let go of my thinking, I told God, "You know why I am here and what I am here to do. You know how much I need and when I need it. I am not going to worry."

"I am not going to worry" became my tool for letting go of worry and fear. It may sound too simple and easy to work. But it did work! And it continues to work. You can try it too!

I want to make this clear: The anxiety and worry were still there, but as soon as I felt the danger of these feelings taking control over me, I would look up and mentally repeat, "I am not going to worry." I wanted the Universe to know that I was not standing in the way. I was determined to get the help from the Universe. I was clear that I couldn't do it alone. And I was clear that the *Universe had a plan.*

Right away something happened. I received a letter in the mail from my mortgage company saying that my monthly payments were going down. I would now pay only half of what I was paying because the interest rates went down. I did not know that could happen. When I told my children who are in the real estate business, they were astounded. I had been paying regularly. I didn't contact the bank to ask for anything; I just let go and I trusted. And the Universe answered, as if telling me, "If you were planning to worry, please don't!"

See? God (the Universe) knows the "how." But we are our worst enemy when we think and worry about money. This is really the worst thing we can do. It isn't any of our business how things will work out, and, when we engage our intellect in finding solutions, we interfere with the Universe.

If you have money problems, the first thing you have to do is stop and breathe. Relax! Let me tell you, I didn't have to fire anyone. I was even able to hire more people. The money ended up coming from places I couldn't ever plan or imagine. It came from publishers around the world who sent me emails proposing to buy the copyright to my books in their own languages. I received invitations for speaking engagements in many countries. We would negotiate, sign a contract and an advance wire transfer would follow. How they all got my email address and became interested in my books and seminars, I have no idea. They would say, "I found you by chance," or, "I found you by accident." Let me tell you, this is what I call God at work.

To be clear, this does not mean that I sit around and don't take action. In fact, I often put in long days. To me, though, what I do does not feel like work. I am following my heart and living my passion, so I am happy to devote time to it. I know "why" I do it. I have a purpose. Opportunities come to me because I am doing what I was meant to do and what I love to do.

Where Do I Start?

Let your profession be the reflection and expression of the best you can give. Do not settle for less. This will trigger the upward spiral of Inspiration, realization, more Inspiration and greater realization, while you prosper financially with little to no effort. People will perceive the energy of your enthusiasm in your work and will want to pay you more money. They won't be able to explain what attracts them to you and your business; they will just feel good around you and will want more of you and your product or service.

Maybe now you work for the sole purpose of earning money and you sacrifice your passion. But I am sure you can see among your customers, providers, friends or family the difference between the people who work for money and those who really love their work. Obviously, those who work doing what they love and what they're passionate about transmit an energy of joy and trust that attracts clients. And their state of joy will continually make them better at what they do, and that in turn will get them even more clients!

So then, what group will you choose to be in? Would you rather be among the worried and unsatisfied people who work mainly for money, relying only on their intellect, and who complain and are dissatisfied most of the time? Or will you be among the happy and inspired people who attract abundance effortlessly? You choose! But remember, if you decide to remain in the first group, your secret is not a secret. People have a sixth sense that makes them feel uncomfortable when they perceive they are working with someone whose only purpose is making money.

Are We Programmed to Fail?

What makes us achieve success against all odds? Why does our business thrive while our competitors' businesses don't, even when the rest of society says we're in a recession and that sales are down? They key to living in full potentiality is practicing an abundant mindset. Let me tell you, what makes the difference is our attitude, what we decide to believe and the actions we take with these attitude and beliefs. We are always "buying" the bad news.

I always say that we were created to be successful but programmed to "fail." We are programmed to believe that things are complicated and difficult, that we have to work hard and prepare ourselves for the rainy days. We are so convinced something bad is going to happen in the future that we need to prepare. We learn that we cannot do what we love, that we need to amass a large retirement account. We must go to the university because an academic title will guarantee us a good job that's going to pay very well and give us security and will make us happy. Is it really so? Did you try it? Are you really happy? Don't have any worries?

Do you see the importance of stopping worrying about the future, of living in the present, taking one moment at a time and enjoying what you do in order to be happy and successful?

During one of my seminars in Asuncion, Paraguay, a woman raised her hand and said, "Mabel, this is great, but we want our children to be honest, hard workers, go to university, become professionals, make money..."

She kept going on and on until I stopped her and said, "Did you realize that your list doesn't include that they'd be happy?"

In a conference in Mexico, a young lady raised her hand and told me: "Mabel, I am going to graduate from high school and I really don't know what career to choose."

My first thought was, *Your mother will not like my response!* The young woman's mother was sitting next to her, so I asked her for permission to speak to her daughter before I answered. Her mother nodded, so I said to the young woman: "Go and travel the world. When you come back, you will know." The whole auditorium applauded. I guess they all shared in her relief and felt liberated.

Similarly, in a seminar in Moscow, Russia, a man asked me, "Mabel, based on what you are saying, do I tell my son not to go to university?"

My response was, "What if your son first finds out who he really is, what his passion is, so he can go to university for the right reasons: to learn more of what he loves and be the best he can be at doing it?"

See, so many of us go to university in order to become "somebody" or to be successful and valued or to obtain security. But ultimately, it is not about degrees. At some time in our lives we decided, consciously or unconsciously, to allow our beliefs to determine our future. For example, we believe we are "somebody" because we have a university degree or we feel inadequate if we don't have one. We are convinced that we know better if we have a university education, assuming that those who are more educated are also more knowledgeable. Well, let me tell you, the more education you have, the further you may be from wisdom or truth, and "the truth shall set you free."

To know *truth*, you need to stop acting based on everything you've learned before, all the knowledge you've acquired. Say, "I love you, but we need to part," to your beliefs, perceptions and expectations and then release them. Show them the other cheek and set yourself free. Truth, same as the state of Zero Frequency®, is an experience. It cannot be described in words. You get there when you are open and willing to admit, "Maybe I don't know as much as I thought I knew." Suddenly you know things *with your heart*. But this knowing has nothing to do with education or learning. It's a natural knowing you cannot explain nor acquire at any school, college or university.

Conecta con ZERO *frequency*

Your happiness is not something outside of you to be obtained; it already exists inside of you. It does not depend on any specific amount of money or success; it does not require recognition or awards. Your happiness is something you choose moment by moment. We need to change our mind-sets about success and money and start practicing abundance. Focus on your inner life first. Once we change our beliefs, the change "out there" is inevitable, because it is a reflection of your inner reality.

Here are a few ways you can experience abundance through connecting to Zero Frequency®:

1. To feel happy instantly, recall moments when you felt joy, when you laughed and laughed, when you danced with glee, when you felt grateful to be alive. Simply revisiting these memories will help you experience that same happiness in your heart again.

2. Remember what Michael Singer says about the importance of letting negative energies such as anger, worry and anxiety "pass right through you." He warns about not storing those energies inside of you. I suggest you repeat mentally: "I am not going to worry."

3. If you find yourself worrying about an uncertain future, repeat mentally, "I let go and trust." Remind yourself that you are on the right path and that the present moment is all you have; in this moment you have everything you need.

4. When you start to question or complain, remind yourself of the big picture: Know why you are doing it. There is always a bigger purpose. Your heart will guide you to your mission.

5. Believe *in you*. Act with confidence. Reconnect with that part of you that knows. You heard this

before: "Fake it till you make it." Trust yourself. Be yourself. Love yourself.

6. Change the conversations in your mind. Realize you can change your thoughts just as you would change the channel on the radio. Replace bad habits with good habits: Instead of thinking and worrying, let go and trust. Instead of listening to your intellect, practice listening to your Inspiration. Tune in to a different station.

7. We all buy into beliefs about money. What you heard about money when you were a child may be controlling the flow of money in your life now. Remind yourself money is only what you believe money is. Practice loving and accepting money in your life. There is nothing wrong with money. Override your negative thoughts by saying, "Thank you, but no thank you; I am busy; I have important things to do." Please know that more is always coming from places you never imagined if you allow it.

8. Creative people will tell you that their ideas don't come from thinking. Are you looking for the million-dollar idea? Do as they did. Connect with nature, go for a walk, listen to music, take a shower

or a nap and be open, because it could come in your dream state. Relax!

You can find more resources on how to go back to Zero Frequency® at *www.zerofrequency.com/bookresources*

Chapter 11

Why It Matters that You Live
at Zero Frequency®

The mind is like a parachute.
It doesn't work unless it's open.
Frank Zappa

Humanity is experiencing different types of upheavals and calamities: tsunamis, earthquakes, fires, floods, air crashes, economic crises, racism, endangered ecosystems, the threat of rising sea levels, human trafficking, the drug epidemic, crime, sexual offenses, terrorist attacks. They ultimately tell us only one thing: this is the moment to wake up.

We must realize that these circumstances are here to help us take responsibility, change and let go of the memories replaying in our minds so we can set ourselves, our communities and the planet free. The change begins with us. If we do not realize this, life is going to become more and more difficult. The Universe is going to hit us harder and harder every time.

The tragedy is that we are still asleep. How many more catastrophes have to happen, and how many more people have to lose their lives, before we wake up? We are so powerful that we can actually destroy everything if we continue to "believe" that peace on Earth is not possible. The world is unstable, and unhappiness is a normal part of life.

Sometimes I set the example of Jesus of Nazareth. He stood up to the Temple because he recognized the power, control and manipulation exerted by the Temple's priesthood over the people. After his death, what did we do? We created Temples in his name! We did not understand any of his powerful messages. My youngest son told me one day: "Mom, you know what I was thinking? If Jesus came back, he would die when he saw what we did in his name."

We are living in an important era of evolution and great changes, and outmoded ways of thinking no longer serve us. We keep telling our children that they are irresponsible if they don't worry. We tell them that they are stupid if they don't think and use their heads. Wake up! That doesn't work. Consciousness is the only way to bring peace to the world. This begins with each of us becoming happy. If you are conscious, your heart is at peace, not at war.

Across the planet, people are waking up to the realization that what used to work no longer does. There is a search for different ways of living. Minds are opening to new possibilities. More and more people realize that they don't know as much as they thought they did. Hopefully they will not resist these realizations! You know, life is hard *because we* resist. We resist everything. We make things so much harder for ourselves.

In a special meditation at an ashram in India, we had to whirl counterclockwise for forty-five minutes. If you did not fall down after whirling, you had to *let* your body fall to the ground. Guess what I found out? If you do not try to plan the landing in advance (control, think, resist), you land softly. The floor absorbs you gently and naturally. When I allowed myself to fall in this way, I felt blending with the earth. Think about it. When children fall, they fall in a relaxed way. They don't try to control the fall; they don't go against it, nor do they try to protect themselves. They do not resist!

Joseph Campbell said, "If you are falling... dive. We are in a freefall into the future. We don't know where we're going. Things are changing so fast, and always when you're going through a long tunnel, anxiety comes along. All you have to do to transform your hell into a paradise is to turn your fall into a voluntary act. It's a very interesting shift of perspective and that's all it is...joyful participation in the sorrows... and everything changes." See, what makes things more difficult for us is that we are resisting (thinking, worrying) all the time. We are going against the flow. In the times in which we are living, we cannot afford to resist anymore.

A new paradigm is upon us. In nearly all aspects of life—from science, to education, to business, and even to our climate—we are realizing that what used to work doesn't work anymore. This is why it is *crucial* that we practice connecting to Zero. Now, more than ever, the planet needs us to be our true selves, free from fear, memories, negativity and perceived limitations. The Universe is calling on all of us to connect with our real identity and go to Zero, for in this limitless, innocent, joyful state, we can rise to the occasion and heal the world.

As the world whirls, allow yourself to fall into the new paradigm. Embrace it and blend with the earth. Do not resist. Go with the flow. Trust the uncertain. Remember, what you resist, persists. Do not be afraid. What is coming is better and greater.

Old Thinking Gives Way to New

In his bestselling book, *The Seven Habits of Highly Effective People,* Steven Covey explains, "The term Paradigm Shift was introduced by Thomas Kuhn in his highly influential landmark book, *The Structure of Scientific Revolutions.* Kuhn shows how almost every significant breakthrough in the field of scientific endeavor is first a break with tradition, with old ways of thinking, with old paradigms."

He goes on to say, "Our Paradigms are the way we 'see' the world or circumstances—not in terms of our visual sense of sight, but in terms of perceiving, understanding, and interpreting. Paradigms are inseparable from character. Being is seeing in the human dimension. And what we see is highly interrelated to what we are. We can't go very far to change our seeing without simultaneously changing our being, and vice versa."

Science is now realizing that many theories, interpretations and assumptions were wrong, or incomplete. One of the pioneers insisting on the need to educate our young people based on different values and principles is Gregg Braden. He graduated from the University of Montana with a BA in geology. This expert in computer systems and researcher of consciousness stresses that we will not be able to solve our problems and challenges based on the old ways of thinking, so the education system must, once and for all, embrace the new trends.

Slowly and surely, people are realizing what a crazy society we have created. We put people in boxes and convert them into ordinary "normal" human beings, and if they don't behave or think accordingly, we medicate them. Aldous Huxley said, "The tendency of the masses is towards mediocrity." Keep focus, keep moving. Do not allow other people's opinion to influence you and make you doubt what your instinct tells you. Are you willing to say "yes" to your gut feelings, even if it means being different?

This year I spoke before twelve hundred high school students in Puebla, Mexico. I was impressed by how they listened to me attentively for ninety minutes. At the end, I asked who wanted to share, ask a question or comment. I was shocked at how many of them came to the stage to share how they related to the message.

I am grateful for the opportunity that God gives me to share with young people. I want to reach as many of them as I can with my message, so they can be happy *now*. While writing this book, I spoke at several high schools in Mexico and Spain and I had more attention from them than I expected. The students shared stories and great testimonies, and I really enjoyed working with them.

In Malaga, Spain, I presented in a high school that some of the more problematic students attend, including some who were expelled from other schools. At the end of my presentation, one student asked me, "And how long does it take to get to Zero?" He was so sweet and sincere. He spoke from his heart. He really wanted to know how to live at Zero Frequency® *now*. I really wanted to hug him.

I told him, "How fast you get to Zero is all up to you. You decide moment by moment. You can be happy now."

Young people are more ready for the new paradigm than you think, and many of them already practice some aspects of what you have learned in this book. They already come with different chips, different perceptions, and they are much more open-minded. Many of them don't have to be told to think "out of the box." They are waiting for *us*. This is why I wrote a children's book, *The Easiest Way to Grow,* for children from three to one hundred years old. (We adults need it as much as children.) In a companion audio to the book, I compiled all the messages that changed my life. We shouldn't have our children go through what we went through, only to find out forty years later that they have wasted their lives. I think it is very important for our kids to be happy NOW.

Thank God a lot of people are reconsidering and are looking at un-schooling and homeschooling their kids. Many kids who've been given such alternative education are now giving amazing talks on the Internet. When you have a moment, look up Logan LaPlante's TEDx University of Nevada talk on how homeschooling makes them happy people.

Spirituality Is the Foundation

A seminar organizer in Japan once asked me why I had not mentioned that my seminars had a spiritual component. I said, "If I did that, no one in the US would hire me."

The organizer replied, "In Japan, we wouldn't hire you unless we knew your seminars had a spiritual component, because in Japan we know that the foundation of a successful business is spirituality."

This is essential. Spirituality is basic and very important. If you remember, I discovered this myself when I was still an accountant and started my journey into what was still very new to me: the spiritual world.

We had a student in California who used to talk to inanimate objects. She was an accountant and one day came to the training and told me that she had quit her job at the accounting firm and would open a flower shop. My first question (my intellect still works very well) was, "But Christine, do you know anything about flowers?"

She said: "No, but I just know I have to do that."

The next training, she came and shared with all of us, saying, "Well, you know… I go to the flower market with my list of orders but, when I get there, I ask the flowers, 'Who is coming with me?' And I see flowers raising their hands. I compare them with my list and notice some that I don't have listed, but I trust and I buy them anyway. As I walk back into the shop, the phone is ringing. I pick up, and the person on the line is asking for those exact flowers that were not on the list but 'raised their hands!'"

This may sound far-fetched, but it is very real for Christine. Why not trust your own instincts? Why not trust your own truth? Do you really need a five-year plan to achieve happiness and abundance? To pursue what interests you, your passions, do you really need a college degree first? There are really no rules, and your reality is your reality.

There are always innovative ideas available. You just have to know how to recognize and channel these ideas. In this way, as we see, even people with "disabilities" can find a stimulating role in society. For example, as of 2017, eighty percent of autistic adults were unemployed.[*] And yet, many autistic people are highly intelligent with skills that some industries look for in new hires, qualities such as attention to detail and creative thinking. In the new paradigm, tech companies such as Microsoft, IBM and Hewlett Packard have seen the value in creating hiring programs for autistic people. These initiatives have also changed the work dynamic for other employees in a positive

---

[*] https://www.monster.com/career-advice/article/autism-hiring-initia-tives-tech

way. Do you see how, when we appreciate the best in each of us, we can move toward a more sustainable and humane society? This is the new paradigm, and you have a part to play in it.

Happiness in the Workplace

The World Happiness Report is a landmark survey of the state of global happiness and is usually released by the United Nations at an event celebrating the International Day of Happiness. The report continues to gain global recognition as governments, organizations and civil societies increasingly use happiness indicators to inform their policy-making decisions. In addition to the rankings, this year's report includes an analysis of happiness in the workplace. It is universally accepted that employees are the backbone of any organization. However, a no less respected source than the Harvard Business Journal acknowledges that *happy* employees—at all levels of hierarchy—are more motivated, productive and committed. .

In the new era we are entering, we are seeing that many businesses are going bankrupt; they are not profitable. Something in them does not work, just as many of our lives do not work. Again, will we continue to make the same choices expecting different results?

We have to open our minds, as individuals and as companies, and create businesses that are in accordance with the new times. And today, the factor of happiness can no longer be ignored. Happiness, in alliance with our individual talents, constitutes the pillar of the new companies and the new world. This shows us also how important it is that we become happy parents, because happy parents raise happy children, and happy children will build happy businesses. Happy businesses don't go bankrupt.

One of the most attended classes at Harvard is a class that offers insight into the secret to happiness. Psychology 1504, or "Positive Psychology," has become the most popular course on campus. And at the University of Pennsylvania, Dr. Martin Seligman talks about authentic happiness. He introduces the scientific foundations of positive psychology and key research findings that lead to a revolutionary understanding of what makes people flourish. In this new paradigm, happiness must be our natural state. This is why it matters that you get to Zero—yes, *you*. When you flourish, others follow, and peace and abundance become our global experience.

Your Place in the New Era

As I said earlier in this chapter, everything is changing. In this new paradigm, the Universe is calling on you to adapt to these changes, to become more flexible with your thinking and your views. The good news is you now know exactly how to do that! When you live in Zero Frequency®, staying open to new ideas and possibilities comes naturally to you, and you are at home in the new paradigm. In fact, you *thrive* in the new paradigm! In this book, I have shared many ways to connect to Zero. This is the easy way to let go of old paradigms in your mind and in your daily life, to rise to the occasion and make the most of the shift that is happening around the world.

Continuous change is a law of the Universe, and it reminds us that all of our circumstances are temporary. This means that whatever challenges we face today can be resolved. There is always a new opportunity for growth, for joy and for peace. You are one hundred percent responsible for your own happiness, abundance and success. When you accept this responsibility and connect to Zero every day, you will not only change your life; you will change the world.

Epilogue

You Have the Right to Make Mistakes

Why do I call these final pages an "epilogue," and not a summary? I use the term epilogue because this is why you read this book—to get to your own epilogue. In the movies, it's the happy life shown months after the lessons are learned and the battles are won. In books, it's the chapter that tells you what happened to the characters you followed long after the story ended. You want a peaceful, abundant, happy epilogue. You want an "after" that celebrates dreams fulfilled. I understand. We all do..

You now know the easiest way to get the epilogue you desire. And yet, for some of you, it may seem to take longer to get to that "after." Sometimes, you will make mistakes. We make mistakes when we want to do things our way, not God's way; when we are sure that we *know*; when we come from intellect, the conscious mind. When you make those mistakes, be gentle with yourself. It's okay. We are humans and we are here to learn. Do the best you can.

Be nice to yourself. Your "mistakes" of the past were part of the learning path. Maybe they were not mistakes at all, but an important part of your preparation. Our greatest learning comes through our adverse experiences. And, I am sure you did the best you could. But now you know you can change that. Now you know how to release what no longer serves you, so you can be happy, at peace and successful.

Thomas A. Edison managed to invent the light bulb after a thousand attempts. Do you think he had the perception that he failed a thousand times? These were his own words: "I didn't fail 1,000 times. The light bulb was an invention with 1,000 steps."

Sometimes difficulties seem insurmountable but, in reality, they are opportunities. Similarly the moments of hard work and sacrifice are the "tests," making sure that the road we're on is the right one for us. If you conclude that "this is not for me," allowing inconvenience or distractions to become an excuse to stop, you may not be following your passion, your path. So maybe it's best to move on. Hearing "no," hitting road blocks—these are opportunities. When this happens to you, just say, "Thank you for the opportunity. Something better is coming." The only failure is when you don't learn.

If you're scared to go for what you want, you probably have not yet touched your soul's true longing or there are too many memories interfering. Only you, in the silence of your heart, can determine what course to follow. Stay true to your heart and do not worry. And as Winston Churchill said: "No matter what happens, never, never, never give up!"

Remember, if you forget to practice, if you leave it behind for a moment, or for months or even years, you can always come back. It's a simple thing, as simple as saying, "I'm sorry. I don't know what I'm doing, but I'm doing my best." It's very important that you are kind to yourself. The Universe will be there, waiting for you, as it was before and as it always will be.

So often, when we make a mistake or stop practicing and letting go, we think we've failed and we punish ourselves. This is human and it is not permanent. You can come back to Zero Frequency® *immediately*. Relax. Stop. Breathe. Laugh. It's very easy. Instead of lamenting, regretting and staying in the past, you bring yourself back to present. And then you do it again. And again. Memories are playing in your mind all the time, and so you do this moment by moment and breath by breath.

In his book, *The Power of Now,* Eckhart Tolle talks about letting go and staying present. He says, "With practice, the sense of stillness and peace will deepen. You will also feel a subtle emanation of joy arising from deep within; the joy of Being... You are much more alert, more awake than in the mind identified state. You are fully present... There is a certain criterion by which you can measure your success in this practice: the degree of peace that you feel within."

The epilogue that will bring you the most peace, abundance and happiness may surprise you. You may envision one "happy ending," and discover, through practice, through following your heart, that *your* true joy is on the path itself. Relax. It will come. And it will be perfect—*for you.*

This is not the day after yesterday. This is the day before tomorrow. This is the first day of your journey to a new life. You have all the tools you need now. No more waiting. It's all up to you. Just trust and take the first step with absolute certainty. Zero Frequency® is the path of least effort.

I know you are ready to find your true self, and to find meaning in your life; that is why you read this book. My wish for you is that you will chose to open your mind and change your perception, that you will enjoy the process and stay present, that you will live in hope with confidence and enthusiasm and that you will trust—and that you will have peace beyond understanding.

About the Author

Mabel Katz is an author, public speaker and internationally acclaimed world peace ambassador. She is recognized as a leading authority of Ho'oponopono, the ancient Hawaiian art and practice of problem-solving for achieving happiness and peace. She is also the creator of Zero Frequency®, a way of life which teaches 100% responsibility, forgiveness, and gratitude as a pathway to Zero—the state in which we free ourselves from restrictive memories and limiting beliefs so that we may discover our inner talents in pursuit of a more abundant life.

Honored with the prestigious 2012 Mil Milenious de Paz Peace Flag, acknowledging her global peace initiative, *Peace Within Is World Peace,* Mabel was officially recognized as one of the world's pre-eminent peace ambassadors, and on January 1, 2015, was awarded the prestigious Public Peace Prize. She has spoken in front of national senates and other influential government bodies, including the United Nations in Vienna, where she launched her internationally acclaimed Peace Begins with Me campaign. In 2013, she was recognized for her humanitarian works by being knighted in the venerable Order of the Orthodox Knights Hospitaller of St. John—Russian Grand Priory, bestowing upon her the title of *Dame Mabel Katz.*

Mabel continues to travel extensively throughout the world, helping countless people find inner peace and greater fulfillment in their lives.

Mabel has also authored several books, which have been translated to more than 20 languages.

When she is not conducting workshops around the world, Mabel brings her unique brand of awareness to prison inmates, special needs children, and dozens of corporations seeking to achieve peak performance through deeper self-awareness.

To find out more about Mabel's life-changing Zero Frequency Programs® for children, parents and educators, to inquire about her full line-up of workshops, seminars and conferences, or to order books, you can contact the author at:

ZERO *frequency*

P.O. Box 427
Woodland Hills, CA 91365
Telephone/Fax: (818) 668-2085
support@mabelkatz.com

Made in the USA
Middletown, DE
30 November 2020